S. Hussain Zaidi is a veteran investigative, crime and terror reporter with a career spanning decades. His previous books include *Mafia Queens of Bombay, Dongri to Dubai, Byculla to Bangkok, Mumbai Avengers* and *R.A.W. Hitman*, some of which have been adapted into popular Bollywood films. Hussain Zaidi lives with his family in Mumbai.

THE DANGEROUS DOZEN

THE DANGEROUS DOZEN

Hitmen of the Mumbai Underworld

S. HUSSAIN ZAIDI

SIMON & SCHUSTER

London · New York · Sydney · Toronto · New Delhi

First published as *The Dirty Dozen*, 2017
This edition published by Simon & Schuster India, 2024

1 3 5 7 9 10 8 6 4 2
Simon & Schuster India
818, Indraprakash Building,
21, Barakhamba Road,
New Delhi 110001

Simon & Schuster: Celebrating 100 Years of Publishing in 2024

www.simonandschuster.co.in

Paperback ISBN: 9788197278952
eBook ISBN: 978-81-972789-2-1

Typeset in India by SÜRYA, New Delhi
Printed and bound in India by Replika Press Pvt. Ltd.

For Dr Sharat Kolke
My friend of 30 years and a benefactor

Gabriel Khan was an esoteric byline that was created to partner with my name. The idea was that Gabriel Khan would have the freedom to talk about facets of journalism which under my personal byline might not sound right. Gabriel Khan was my alter ego.

Much later, when I presented the book to my friend Dr Sharat Kolke, whom I have dedicated the book to, he pointed out the existence of real Gabriel Khans, one a British photographer and the other a German cardiologist. We had a good laugh over it.

I must thank filmmaker and storyteller Neeraj Pandey who agreed to write a foreword at short notice, and a special thanks to Mohsin Rizvi whose brilliant visualization got us a knockout cover for this book.

S. Hussain Zaidi

CONTENTS

INTRODUCTION vii

PROLOGUE: A Gangster's Lair 1

HITMAN 1: The Power of a Prawn-like Physique 17

HITMAN 2: The Jettisoned Official Killer 35

HITMAN 3: Blood Guzzling Bagga 54

HITMAN 4: The Maya of Mobsters 67

HITMAN 5: The Mama of Maharashtrian Mafia 88

HITMAN 6: The Ghost Who Killed 106

HITMAN 7: Boyhood to Bhaidom 125

HITMAN 8: From Political Assassin to Padre 147

HITMAN 9: Bulletproof Bora Becomes Baba 163

HITMAN 10: The Saga of Sunil and Sulaiman 185

HITMAN 11: Dhanda, Danda and Dawood 204

EPILOGUE: Gunmen's Gaffes 220

INTRODUCTION

I started my career in journalism at a time when typewriters were treasured and when newsrooms were not cold, clinical, impersonal cabins with corporate trappings. The newsrooms of my time were huge with an open plan area. There were tennis table-size wooden desks, one for the reporting team and another for the editing team. A long row of benches was where the reporters sat and typed away their copies on Godrej typewriters. There was a place for the teleprinter, from where we got the wires, PTI, UNI, Reuters. And yes, we also had a tribe called proof-readers, who were the last in the news food chain. No gaffe escaped their sharp eyes. The features desk were lucky fellas who generally got cabins and lived life kingsize with only weekly Sunday pages to fill. They didn't have to produce two stories a day, or so we thought.

The newsrooms were always messy, with lots of papers, notebooks, and printouts. The journalists hung their jhola bags from their plastic woven wooden chairs or metal chairs woven with plastic. Typewriters were at a premium and there was a mad scramble for non-defective ones with all their keys intact. If you were lucky to start your career at the training ground, *The Free Press Journal* or *Indian Express*, the sea view was a bonus. When the muse didn't work, one could always find inspiration in the angry turbid Arabian Sea that was pushed into a corner at the end of Free Press Journal Marg in Nariman Point.

There were a couple of black rotary dial phones in the room, but you could make a call only if the telephone operator—seated in her lofty cabin near the entrance—deigned to connect your number. You had to keep the telephone operator very happy. Direct phone lines were only for the editor and, sometimes, the chief reporter. You could chain-smoke in the newsroom and both male and female journalists puffed away to glory. The chaiwallah was always being summoned for endless cups of tea punctuated with bhajjis and sandwiches. And the chaiwallah was always asking for money and the journalists were always broke.

Some journalists wore long kurtas and jeans, while others wore shirts that were never tucked into their pants. Most male journalists had a moustache and a beard or a stubble. You would find only a handful of clean-shaven ones. They looked like poets and spoke with the air of one having to carry the burden of mankind on their shoulders. The female journalists cut their hair into a very short crop and were strong-willed. They, too, loved khadi and were always informally dressed. And yes, they wore sarees too.

Newsrooms transitioned to computers within two years of my new career in journalism, and the now defunct *Indian Post* was the first paper to get Atex computers which, in the late '80s, had military applications. Reporters could send messages to each other on their computers, the first version of Gmail chats. And yes, it was the era of newspaper clippings and libraries for background research. Sans Google, journalism was none the poorer.

It was an era when journalists were not discriminatory in what they read. It was an eclectic choice of reading material: Aleksandr Solzhenitsyn, Graham Greene, Jane Austen, Roald Dahl, Agatha Christie and Jeffrey Archer.

I loved the feel and pulse of journalism and I never thought beyond it. There was something magical about it. The feeling that we were instruments of social change and that we had a responsibility to society and mankind. That we were not mere chroniclers of our times, but shaped opinions and changed perceptions and that our pen was actually mightier than the sword. (The disillusionment came much later, with age and wisdom.)

In the late '80s, when I started my career in journalism, journalists were an intrepid lot. They wrote stories that could bring down governments. Arun Shourie had ripped apart A. R. Antulay in the cement scam, and Maneck Davar exposed the link between Dhirubhai Ambani's Reliance Industries and the Central Bureau of Investigation director Mohan Katre. (Davar posed as a small scale detergent manufacturer and entrapped Katre's son Umesh into revealing his business dealings with Reliance.) It was an era when journalists wrote in shorthand but were not stenographers. It was when movies reflected the times we lived in, like *Saaransh* and *Ardh Satya*. There was no political censure and no censor.

It was a time when journalists were sceptical about politicians and their intent. For journalists, the establishment was always to be questioned. The politicians were always the snake in the grass. Pakistan was a country that got separated at birth. We watched *Tamas* with pain in our hearts. We were not at war with Pakistan every day, as television channels now are. And that was because we focused on the here and now. We had local issues and starvation, poverty, bad infrastructure, poor governance, corruption, tribal issues, zilla parishad scams, farmers' problems, communal riots, the Bhopal gas tragedy, a burning Punjab, Kalahandi and Bhagalpur. It was a time when the Page 3 social scene idea was just incubating in some party-hopper's mind.

It was a time when the great Vinod Mehta turned the definition of investigative and interesting journalism on its head. The *Sunday Observer* was a trail-blazing newspaper. It shook the behemoth, especially the Old Lady of Boribunder.

I started writing on crime occasionally, while covering other beats. Crime reporting was challenging because getting contacts was not easy unless one wanted to report only the police version. When I met S. Hussain Zaidi, he was a promising young man, all of twenty-seven, shy and reserved. He was heavily into reading paperbacks and was very promising. His narrative skills were in place even at that formative stage in his life. I thought he should be taken under my wing. Over several bun maskas at Yazdani Bakery in Fort, and gallons of carrot juice, Hussain's destiny and future was shaped as the top crime journalist of Mumbai.

When I moved to television for a year, Hussain established himself as a crime reporter of much merit at the *Indian Express,* which had just launched its city supplement under Sai Suresh Sivaswamy. It was called the *Express Newsline*. Hussain's stories were creating waves and the Rotary Club had already invited him as a guest. He spoke on 'How not to fear the dreaded extortion call'.

Since we were never in competition we became buddies and in him I discovered a hungry protégé. With experience and subsequent success, he built better contacts and collected more scoops. In the early days, he was very humble and did not think it beneath him to touch my feet even in public on Guru Purnima. He once bent and touched my feet in a public square at Matunga Circle.

My crime contacts were virtual encyclopaedias and had more archived facts in the recesses of their brains than the Mumbai police had in their dog-eared dossiers. Sadly, most of them have been felled by death. A few I can name. The late chief of the Anti Terror Squad (ATS) Hemant Karkare, Customs Inspector Farooq Batatawala, Deputy Commissioner of Police Deepak Jog, ganglord Hussain Shaikh alias Ustara, Dilawar Khan, killed at twenty-eight, and Badshah, who I think is still alive. I introduced Hussain to my sources back then, and he was an instant hit with them.

Though Hussain and I held divergent points of view on most topics, we were bound together by our shared common destiny—crime reporting.

In his journalistic career, Hussain unravelled the Mumbai mafia like no other journalist has ever done. He also shattered many myths. He belied the celluloid notion of the archetypal gunman as a heroic, dauntless fellow with reckless audacity. He gave the gunman a name, a face and painted them in real colours, a far cry from their virtual persona. He told us that in real life they were not at all heroic. That some of them were feckless, while others could not even shoot straight. That the ones who killed recklessly were also psychos. And the ones who aimed straight with their guns were not necessarily brave but bolstered by the weapon in their hand. Hussain's story, 'Gangster's Shame Cannot Cock a Gun', which was carried as a lead story in the *Express Newsline*, is a case in point. It was the first article on crime that took a derisive line and denigrated mafia hitmen. The mafia across the board were not at all amused by that story.

Like some Mantralaya journalists, crime reporters tend to take sides. Some become spokespersons for certain mafia groups. Both the police and mafia informers become very wary of such reporters. Once when we went to Peon Chawl at Byculla to meet Arun Gawli's shooter, Raju Phillips, he was astonished to learn that we do not take money. Raju ratted out several names of journalists, especially from the regional press, who were on their steady payroll. On the other hand, Hussain's credo was 'Roti sirf reporting se'.

The mafia gangs, therefore, held him in high esteem, even when he wrote adversely about them and exposed them! He was never labelled as 'us gang ka aadmi'. They came after him for various reasons (like exposing a ganglord's affair with his lieutenant's wife), but never for his sympathies and affiliations with other gangs. It was for this reason that he could step into Kolhapur jail (to meet Gawli) with as much aplomb as he could walk into a Karachi hideaway (to meet Dawood's acolytes). Hussain managed to have contacts in most of the top gangs, including Dawood, Chhota Shakeel, Abu Salem, Chhota Rajan and even Arun Gawli. Then there was the P gang. The Mumbai police force.

Despite his seething resentment of the Mumbai police force and its wicked ways, Hussain has often put them on a pedestal and elevated the men in uniform to a heroic stature. In all his books, right from *Black Friday*, *Dongri to Dubai* and *Byculla to Bangkok*, his books showcase the exploits of the Mumbai police, at times a bit exaggerated in my opinion.

Since Hussain is very prolific, he has almost written on all shades of crime. While reading his books, I felt I could write about the men who wielded the gun for the dons. The hitmen might seem lowly in their stature as they are more of a tool to be used and thrown or killed by the police or rivals, but some of them have gone on to shape a gang's trajectory. The profiles included in this book are of some of these bloodthirsty and violent men; a few of them were drawn by the lure of the lucre, while others were drawn by a belief in their invincibility.

Those who pitched in were Gautam Mengele, Nazia Sayed and Jyoti Shelar. While Nazia is already a published author, Gautam is prepping himself to be one.

We also took the help of a bright, young student of St. Xavier's called Raina Bhagat. All of twenty, Raina showed tremendous promise, professionalism and dedication to the work assigned to her.

Jyoti Shelar gave much of her time while she was in the midst of her own maiden book, *The Bhais of Bengaluru*. And she never batted an eyelid when I asked her to finish my task first before flying off to various cities in Karnataka for her research work.

Through these young professionals, I would also like to extend my thanks to their sources and friends who were of tremendous help in fleshing out the characters in the book.

I would like to thank retired assistant commissioner of police Jaywant Hargude and ACP Sunil Deshmukh of Dadar division.

Gabriel Khan

PROLOGUE

A Gangster's Lair

I was overcome with obsessive interest in my subject for months. And yet, when I first saw him, it was a shocking disappointment. Looks can be deceptive they say, but the man standing in the room across from me looked nothing like a sharpshooter of his reputation. He was short and stout; the makings of a potbelly and stooping shoulders gave him an awkward hunch. He was wearing the all-white look one tends to see in the underworld. Tailored white shirt, white pants and white shoes, I couldn't check his socks, but I bet they were white too.

He had a decent haircut and a direct stare. I didn't like his eyes though. His eyes were those of an arrogant and boastful man. His stance was firm but his diminutive personality failed to arouse any terror in me. He reminded me of the famous Bollywood singer Udit Narayan minus the *pahadi* voice and the skin colour. But this Udit Narayan of the underworld was a man known more for his skills with the gun and proficiency with a blade. The blade runner.

There was a bank of closed circuit television screens

behind the man, hitched to several hidden cameras. Obviously he had watched me come up the street. Since I had already set foot in his lair, I resolved to make the meeting count. He rose to greet me with proper Islamic customs and mannerisms. In a husky yet powerful voice, he said, 'My name is Mohammed Hussain Shaikh, but they call me Ustara.' He spoke in colloquial Urdu.

My curious eyes scanned him head to toe, and stopped at the sight of two guns holstered in his pants. The guns peeked out of their holsters, and induced a slight intimidation in me. My glance immediately shifted away from Ustara to the table that separated us. I spotted three mobile phones carelessly lying next to a pile of papers. In those days, apart from BPL, Max Touch was the most prominent service provider, and cell phone technology had just been introduced in Mumbai. A call from a mobile phone was priced at nothing less than Rs. 36 per minute; the same charges applied to incoming calls as well. At a time when most citizens like me could barely afford one phone, Ustara was flaunting three. 'One is for my *jaan*, one for my family, and the third one for the business,' he quipped. His 'jaan'—a euphemism for his current love interest.

It was Farooq Batatawala, inspector from the Marine and Preventive Wing of the Customs department who introduced me to Hussain Ustara. Ustara was a gangster who hated Dawood's Man Friday, Chhota Shakeel. He didn't like their remote control method of extortion. 'You can't sit in Dubai and make threatening calls to people from there and then send your boys to do the dirty job.

We do the same thing but we sit in Mumbai and face the pressures,' he would say.

He was also the first hitman I met in the mafia, and perhaps that was why I was fascinated by him. Ustara was the ring leader of a small group of gunmen who were operating from Pydhonie in south Mumbai. His hideout was a rundown building on Bapu Khote Street. The entire building belonged to Ustara. He also had a close-knit group of five to six people who worked for him and kept Ustara informed about the affairs of the area.

I almost missed the entrance to Ustara's rundown building twice. There are shops on the ground floor and as you make your way to the first floor via a narrow flight of stairs, there is a huge empty room that seems like an abandoned warehouse on the left—or is it a Fire Refuge floor, I wondered. It was pitch dark and cavernous as I proceeded upstairs.

Though he eventually became well known for his guns, his clever use of razor blades in his formative teenage years had earned him the title of Ustara. He was adept at flashing the ustara, barber's knife, at the right moment and at the right target. Ustara narrated the story to me. In his teens, he was part of a gang of pickpockets and was hauled up by his ringleader for not depositing the entire day's earnings. The man, who was a bully, was heavily-built and broad-shouldered like a giant, clearly an oversized opponent for the sixteen-year-old Ustara. There was a skirmish and Ustara was cornered by the ringleader's minions. In desperation and armed with nothing but a blade and unmatched valour, he attacked the man, slashing his neck and drawing the blade down to his navel and below. The doctor at the hospital who treated the injured man remarked that the person who cut him had done so with surgical precision.

The man survived, but Ustara became famous in the inner circles of the Mumbai underworld as the boy who could use an ustara to settle arguments. From that time, the weapon had become synonymous with him, and hence the name. He showed me the razor he was carrying in his sleeve. Whenever trouble approached, or if circumstances pushed Ustara into a fistfight, he would merely dig into his sleeve and then the penetrative slash would follow. Some really deft criminals in jails can hide blades in their mouths.

Ustara also took great pride in his skills with all kinds of weapons. He boasted of being able to assemble and shoot a gun in less than three seconds flat. A feat otherwise only portrayed in mafia movies. I particularly remember one scene in *The New Police Story,* where the ageing and washed-out cop, played by Jackie Chan, would lose to a nimble-fingered younger gunman who was always faster and quicker. Ustara was agile like no gunmen ever heard of, and at the same time he could use his trademark weapon to bring death upon his opponents. But he admitted that he loved guns more, his favourite being the Mauser pistol (1914 model)—the authentic German model, not the Chinese one, which is actually a cheaper imitation of the original.

Ustara said he managed to stay out of trouble with the cops, as he was an informer and gave a lot of valuable information on the underworld in exchange for his freedom. He rattled off some names of top cops, but I could never independently verify his claims. He mentioned that he had a very special knack of judging and employing people, which others lacked. Ustara's close group of trusted men had six members, each suffering from some deformity. Ustara believed that when a man was disabled in any manner, god would compensate him by blessing him with an alternative, sharpened sense. Ustara signalled, and his sidekicks emerged out of the woodwork, literally—the walls seemed to have no doors. The gang members were all in their late thirties. They seemed to have lived a tough life. Their faces were scarred and they all looked like they had been thoroughly whiplashed by life. He introduced me to all his gang members and I noticed that all of them sported a deformity or an unusual feature. Some had an extra appendage, one had different coloured eyes, another had one big ear. Even the resident cat had one grey and one amber eye, both holding a malevolent glare. 'People with deformities have other acute senses. They are very good in my line of work,' he reiterated.

One man in his group had the unique ability to detect a cross-connection on any phone call. Another member could lip-read conversations of people from across the street with precision. It was with the expedient use of the skills of his group coupled with his impressive leadership that Ustara combated Dawood Ibrahim for more than eight years and survived.

Ustara took me to the first floor room, which I'd

initially thought was a Fire Refuge. The walls of the room were riddled with bullet holes. 'Practice makes perfect,' he said. So the floor was actually a space for target practice.

The Meeting of Two Hussains

A few days later, I introduced Ustara to the budding crime journalist at *Indian Express*, Hussain Zaidi, who was accompanied by his mentor and friend Vikram Chandra, the internationally famous author of several bestselling books, including *Love and Longing in Bombay*, *Red Earth and Pouring Rain* and *The Sacred Games*. Ustara left a lasting impression on both men. However, while Hussain Zaidi was fascinated with the exploits and bravado of Ustara, it was the inner workings of the gangster's complex mind that caught the attention of Vikram Chandra. As Zaidi later told me, Vikram noticed the cologne that Ustara wore. Despite being a gangster with no schooling and one who couldn't speak two sentences in English, Ustara took delight in telling them that he was wearing Paco Rabanne. Later, when both the friends were walking towards their vehicle, Hussain asked Vikram what he thought was the most striking thing about the gunman's personality, to which the famous and articulate author said:

'What struck me was that his intelligence really showed in how good a "crime consultant" he was for me when we meet. Often, your informant or interview will meander around the subject; they will go off on tangents, they will actually start explaining something other than what you asked about. Ustara, in contrast, provided a concise but complete explanation of whatever I asked him about. He had an analytical bent of mind, so I could ask him—for instance—about the ground-level activities that somebody could use to steal an election, and he was able to give me a complete breakdown of the resources required, the various steps taken to achieve victory, etc.'

Hussain admired and noted down Vikram's observation. Vikram had showed similarly sharp perception when the duo had visited Pathan gang's chieftain Karim Lala's Tahir Manzil house in Baida Gully near Novelty Cinema on Grant Road in the late '90s. Karim Lala was almost ninety years old then. While leaving the building, Vikram was drawn to an enormous painting on the wall. The picture depicted a ferocious tiger preying on a very meek and vulnerable deer. Vikram noticed that the painting was a projection of the mindset of a man who took extreme pleasure in intimidating his victims, owing to the strength and power that he possessed.

Karim Lala and Ustara were similar in their domineering personalities. Ustara had managed to unleash terror on the entire Bapu Khote Street and Pydhonie area: people were simply terrified of this gangster in their midst. Every occurrence on the street was reported to Ustara. He was the sole point for regulation and control, and thereby held the reins of power for the area. Ustara was also extremely brave, despite being the leader of a very small gang. He had the daring to defy anyone who stood in his way, including Dawood Ibrahim, the only major don of that era.

He had the bravura of a gangster and his pride often overlapped with complacent conduct. He liked to paint himself as a hero of sorts. And, as we saw later, this was customary behaviour for every other gangster—they liked to indulge in self-aggrandizement, relating their own stories in extraordinary terms.

Zaidi met Ustara a number of times in the coming months, and they advanced from being acquaintances to becoming friends. Ustara opened up about his sexual escapades. He also told Zaidi tales of Sapna didi, which Zaidi incorporated in his best-selling novel *Mafia Queens of Mumbai*. He also let Zaidi delve into the deeper details of his life—his growth and the circumstances and choices that led him to becoming the gangster that he was. He unmasked himself to Zaidi and divulged to him the deepest secrets of his life and trade.

Zaidi would take notes of these insightful conversations with Ustara and, once back home, he would weave them into his stories.

Before I go further, though, I should write more about Farooq Batatawala, whom I mentioned earlier. He was the one who introduced me to Ustara.

In time, I gifted both these sources to Hussain. Their encyclopaedic insights into the Mumbai mafia made him a better crime journalist and writer in the days to come.

A Potboiler Saga

Farooq's story read like a quintessential Bollywood tale. He had a childhood friend, someone he played *gilli danda* and cricket with. However, as they grew up, they parted ways. While Farooq became a law-enforcing officer, his friend instead chose a different path that led to him becoming an outlaw, a don. This friend was none other than Dawood Ibrahim Kaskar. And, as in a typical Bollywood film, Farooq Batatawala was a conscientious officer who made it his mission to chase down his childhood buddy and bring him to book.

Farooq had harboured a grudge against the khaki; or I surmise that he couldn't land a job with the Mumbai police and so he became a customs officer instead. He was very successful and was seen as something of a legendary officer, but his sole agenda in life remained the persecution of his childhood friend, and it drove him to bust every consignment belonging to Dawood Ibrahim. Farooq was never as consumed by his wife or children or his dire financial situation as much as he was by the need to bring Dawood down and demolish his empire in the city. It was not personal though. Sheer professionalism drove Farooq to put his life out on a limb.

I still remember my first with Farooq.

If the sound of hurtling suburban meeting trains at intervals of three to four minutes was unsettling, so was the man sitting across from me. Farooq was of average Indian height (five foot, ten inches), and was clad in jeans and a denim shirt tucked inside with a big belt around his waist—I was to learn later that he loved denim. We were sitting at a tiny Irani restaurant near the Marine & Preventive Wing of the Customs Department abutting the Marine Lines railway station. The seating arrangement had been his idea: he wanted to sit so he could face the restaurant's entrance. He was not looking at me. He was talking to me, but his attention was on the door. His right hand was always poised near his right leg, which was placed strategically outside the table's legs.

Months later, when we were comfortable with each other and he had begun to trust me, and there were no more distracted looks towards the entrance, he told me about the holster he had wrapped around his boot, and his gun, of course. Unlike Ustara, Farooq had settled for a Chinese Mauser. It took a lot of Coca-Cola, much beating around the bush and several conversations to finally melt the ice. And it was no mean achievement, because the man never trusted anybody.

I was taken aback when I first saw him. A devout Muslim—though he never spoke about religion—he was also a staunch disciplinarian. The only aspect about him that didn't gel with this was his fetish for Coca-Cola, his love for cigarettes and weakness for non-vegetarian oily food, all of which showed on his stomach. His good-looking face was hidden by a big beard, like a mullah, and he had a moustache like a sardarji. Devout Muslims normally trim their moustache to prevent the hair from touching the lips, but he did not care. He was in his early thirties, a modern Muslim, well-educated—from St. Mary's Convent at Mazagaon. He was fair, but the bags under his eyes indicated that he was not sleeping well. In fact, he was an insomniac. His English was fluent, no hiccups. He had a nice smile, but the foliage around his face robbed the smile of depth.

Farooq was a good cop, a damned good and honest cop in a department full of crooks. The Marine & Preventive Wing of the Customs Department was created to counter smuggling activities via the sea. Those were the days when Dawood was very active in smuggling silver, which he occasionally did through the sea route. Though Manmohan Singh had declared our own perestroika and glasnost in 1992, old habits die hard and smuggling as a way of life had yet to lose its appeal.

But like most government departments, there were few people in the Marine & Preventive Wing who had the spunk to take on the might of the smugglers. In fact, many were in collusion with the smugglers and were paid to look the other way. It was very good money, sometimes paid in bars of gold. The only man in the department who cocked a snook at the smugglers was Farooq. And Farooq was a formidable one-man army. He would disappear for days in the sea, in a boat with his Coca-Cola and the Chinese Mauser. Even his buddy in the customs department, Swaminathan, would not be aware of his location. Once, when I asked his wife Shabnam about his whereabouts, she said nonchalantly that he had not come home for several days. That was the norm with Farooq. Shabnam was blasé.

Farooq had managed to torpedo Dawood's smuggling rackets and that had made the don furious. He had neutralized the Pathans in a very violent way and could not believe that he now had adversaries in two such fundamentally different people. One was a resourceful and dedicated customs officer who was using government machinery to launch a crackdown on him, and the other was a gangster with a small group of minions. Dawood wanted both of them dead. He didn't care that Farooq was his childhood friend and that he was simply doing his duty. He thought Farooq was foolhardy to take on the might of the Dawood empire, and not expect to get burned.

Dawood did what he did best. He hatched a good plot to finish off both his detractors. His first target was Ustara. Dawood knew Ustara was a womanizer. Despite being married and the father of several children, Ustara was known to have multiple extramarital affairs. So he decided to plant a woman in Ustara's life. This strategy had worked for Dawood with other gangsters, including Samad Khan.

After Sapna didi's gruesome murder in 1994, Ustara had stopped chasing women. However, he was completely smitten with the new entrant in his life. Their relationship carried on for weeks and Ustara remained totally oblivious to her underlying agenda. It was then that Ustara's lady love pleaded with him to meet her in private and convinced him not to bring his bodyguards with him. She said she didn't want anyone to know they were meeting; it would stop people from talking about them or getting suspicious. Since Ustara was completely besotted, he gave in.

The Epitaph

On a clear, sunny day in 1998, during one of Ustara's visits to his lady love, Dawood's right-hand man Chhota Shakeel sent an army of his assailants to gun Ustara to death. Shakeel knew it would take more than a few men to take Ustara down. The six gunmen assigned to the job by Shakeel packed themselves into three cars and on three bikes for the mission. The men were armed to the teeth—they did not want to leave any scope for Ustara surviving the attack.

On that day, an unsuspecting Ustara stepped out of his lover's house only to be greeted by half a dozen gunmen. As soon as he stepped out into the open and headed for his bike, he was hit by a volley of bullets. There stood a man who boasted of assembling a dismantled gun and loading it in less than three seconds, staring death right in the eye as bullet after bullet hit his convulsing body. The post-mortem reports said twenty-seven bullets had pierced through his frame. The gunmen disappeared, and his killers were never found.

In his day, Ustara had been an inside informer for several crime branch officers and helped them crack many cases. However, in death, Ustara had no visitors from the crime branch. Neither was there any investigative effort into finding Ustara's killers.

When Hussain and I visited Ustara's grave, he recalled what Ustara had told Vikram, when asked, 'Where do you see your life going? Will you ever retire?'

Ustara had said sardonically, 'I have dug graves for

many people. Someone will dig a *khadda* (grave) for me.' And here we were—two crime journalists who had got several stories from this man—standing by his grave.

After Ustara's death, there was one more man left to be taken care of by Dawood Ibrahim. His childhood friend, Mohammed Farooq Batatawala. Dawood first wanted to usurp from Farooq his most prized possession—his custom officer's uniform. Thus, he manipulated a situation so that Farooq got into a fight with a local gangster named Dilawar Khan.

The two men knew each other, but nobody knows why or how Dilawar managed to get under Farooq's skin one day after Friday prayers. During the course of the fight, Dilawar aggravated and provoked Farooq to a boiling point of rage, to which Farooq whipped out his gun from his boot and shot Dilawar dead. Dilawar's death resulted in Farooq's arrest by the Mumbai police and he was thrown into lock-up. During his custody in the Crime Branch lock-up at the police headquarters at Crawford Market, Hussain Zaidi once paid him a visit. When asked by Zaidi if there was anything he needed, Farooq sheepishly responded, 'Two-three bottles Coke *pila do*.'

An emotionally-moved Zaidi decided to fulfil his friend's wish. I still remember that scene—I was watching from the windows of the police press room. In the midst of all the officers and lawyers, we could see Zaidi carrying eight large bottles of Coke for his friend and source. Farooq was overwhelmed when he saw Zaidi carrying so many bottles for him. Zaidi also had to coax the Crime Branch officer present to allow Farooq to have all those bottles in his cell.

Farooq spent several months in jail, and consequently—as per the service rules—was suspended from his duties. When he returned, Farooq was a completely bitter man. He felt cheated by the Mumbai police, whom he had selflessly helped during the 1993 blasts, only to be abandoned by them in the time of his own need. The police hadn't reciprocated his favours. Farooq narrated to us countless incidents that he witnessed during his incarceration in jail, of men languishing for years in prison after being falsely implicated by the police.

Although Farooq was released on bail, he did not have any security. Financially he was in dire straits, and his department had begun treating him like a pariah. His weapon was taken away and he was left without the secure cloak of being a customs officer. The incident and the following year in prison left Farooq vulnerable, much to the pleasure of the mastermind behind it all, Dawood Ibrahim.

A few weeks after his release from jail on bail, Chhota Shakeel sent his men to shoot Farooq dead. Farooq and his wife had just stepped out of a telephone booth when he spotted the killers. His hand reflexively went towards his non-existent gun, but he knew his time was up. He saw death in the face of the man who shot him.

After his jail term, Farooq once said, '*Sadrakhsnay khalnigrahnay* (to protect good and destroy evil), the leitmotif of the Mumbai police, is meant only for movies. In real life, the cops always do the opposite.'

Farooq didn't die instantly. There is a way in which the state machinery and the police kill people they don't like. They just let them die. J J Hospital, which is state-run and where the police have the last word, was told to simply not touch Farooq. A physically-strong man like Farooq was left to bleed on a stretcher outside the casualty ward at the hospital—there were no ostensible efforts to save him. The city administration conveniently ignored all the services he had rendered, often risking his life in the process. Ironically, even Dilawar Khan, the man Farooq had shot, died lying unattended at J J Hospital.

And thus, like the innumerable other victims of Dawood's vengeance, Ustara and Farooq both had deaths they never saw coming. However, these men provided us journalists with fantastic stories. Their vibrant insights into the Mumbai underworld will be immortalized in books and articles, as we try and understand the shooters, the gunmen and the contract killers through the eyes of the insiders of the Mumbai underworld.

HITMAN 1

The Power of a Prawn-like Physique

The street bustled with activity as hawkers called attention to their wares, each one competing to be a little louder than the next man. The long, traffic-filled street was lined with everything that money could buy. Tea, fast food, sweetmeats, clothes, watches, sunglasses, undergarments, belts, wallets and jewellery jostled for the attention of the scores of people walking up and down.

As the muezzin's call wafted into the small, two-room apartment in Pydhonie from a nearby mosque, its single occupant raised himself off the bed and unrolled a small mat on the floor. Putting on a skull cap, he knelt down on the mat and closed his eyes. Normally, he would have gone to the nearest mosque to offer namaaz. But he had strict instructions not to step out of the apartment unless absolutely necessary. The instructions had come directly from the chief enforcer of the largest, most dreaded gang in Mumbai's underworld. And the young man of diminutive build was nothing if not a loyal member of the gang. If Chhota Shakeel told him to do something, he did it without asking questions.

Brawl with a Bully

His real name was Syed Muzakkir Mudassar Hussain. But nobody called him that anymore. Elders in his family called him Munna. Others called him Munna bhai. The police called him Jhingada, which means prawn-like. Nicknamed thus out of contempt because of his small frame and scrawny physique, Munna Jhingada had ensured that the name was now taken with fear and respect, instead of the derision with which it had been bestowed on him.

Born in Janata Colony in Jogeshwari (East), Jhingada grew up with his parents and two siblings reading and hearing about the exploits of gangsters like Haji Mastan and Varadarajan Mudaliar. By the time he was a teenager, they had been replaced by Dawood Ibrahim Kaskar and his right-hand man, Shakeel Babumiyan Sheikh, alias Chhota Shakeel.

Like any other teen of his age in the 1990s, Jhingada strutted through the bylanes of his locality with three to four of his friends, pretending to be *bhais* of their own little domains. Fear was for losers and walking away from fights was suicide for their street cred. Fights, and the scars they left you with, were badges of honour to be flaunted, and even the occasional thrashing delivered by his father, a humble plumber by trade, did not deter Munna from his *bhaigiri*.

The endless stories of the D-gang's exploits, fuelled by flamboyant portrayals of gangsters in Bollywood movies, further stoked Jhingada's ambition and he would always be on the lookout for another fight, another proverbial scalp to add to his belt. What neither Jhingada nor his hapless parents ever imagined in their wildest dreams was where he would end up one day.

Jhingada's journey down the bloody path began one afternoon in 1991, when he was a second year Bachelor of Arts student in Ismail Yusuf College in Jogeshwari. He was entering the college campus with two of his classmates when another student named Wazir called out to him. Wazir was among the several bullies in the college who liked to sit near the college gate with his cronies and pretend that he was running a fiefdom. In Jhingada's mind, Wazir was little more than a brawny idiot. He had never had any respect for Wazir, and was not about to start giving him any.

When Wazir ordered him to come over to where he was standing, Munna coolly stood where he was and told Wazir to come over himself. Munna's friends went cold at this open challenge to the college bully's supremacy, but Munna did not display as much as a twitch on his face.

'*Chutiye, bola na, idhar aa!*' Wazir roared at him.

'*Behra hai kya? Suna nahi maine tujkho bola idhar aa?*' Munna responded.

A furious Wazir stormed over to Munna, his shirt tails flapping up and down, the chopper he had stuck in the waistband of his jeans clearly visible. Munna's two friends started backing away at the sight of the blade, but Munna did not move an inch.

Wazir reached the spot where Munna was standing with his hands on his hips and shoved the latter in the chest. Munna responded by pushing back. A stunned Wazir could only say, 'Do you realize who you are messing with? Do you see the bloody chopper I have? I'll carve you up!'

In response, Munna reached out, whipped the dagger out of Wazir's waistband, and drove it into his chest. Wazir stumbled backwards, blood spouting from his chest as if from a fountain, while the crowd of students who had gathered around the two boys in anticipation of witnessing a good fight, backed away in mute horror.

When the onlookers finally wrapped their heads around the fact that the nineteen-year-old Arts student had stabbed someone in broad daylight, the girls started screaming. A young boy went to the pavement and puked his guts out. Within seconds, only Munna and his two friends were standing at the spot, while Wazir lay on the ground, blood and life ebbing out of his twitching body, his eyes mirroring his shock at being attacked in his own domain with his own weapon.

Jhingada calmly turned around to his friends and told them, '*Sab ko bolna, Jhingada ne maara Wazir ko. Abbu ko bolna mai surrender hone jaa raha hoon.* (Tell everyone that it was Jhingada who killed Wazir. And tell my father I'm going to surrender to the police.)'

Jhingada went straight to the Jogeshwari police station, where word of the murderous attack on a college student had just reached, someone having called the police control room and the control room having relayed the information to them. A team was leaving for the spot when Jhingada walked in and told them that he had stabbed a boy in his college. The cops could only stare at the chit of a teen in front of them for a full minute before one of them regained control of his motor impulses and led him to the lock-up.

Still stunned, the duty officer called up his immediate boss, the zonal Deputy Commissioner of Police (DCP), to inform him that the accused in a sensational assault case had just walked into the police station to surrender. The DCP jumped into his vehicle and rushed to the police station to personally interrogate the young man.

Two hours later, the DCP walked out of the detection room of the police station wearing a look of amazement on his face. 'Not a trace of regret!' he told the Senior Police Inspector of the police station. 'Not a trace! He says he wants to be let out so that he can finish the job. Keep a close eye on the bastard.'

Meanwhile, Wazir was rushed to a nearby hospital where he succumbed to his injuries a couple of hours later. The case of attempt-to-murder against him was upgraded to murder just hours after it was registered. Munna Jhingada had tasted blood for the first time.

A month later, Jhingada was released on bail, his lawyer finally succeeding in convincing the magistrate that he had no past record and was not a flight risk. His father took him home, sat him down, and made it clear to him that he was not going to let his eldest son throw his life away. Jhingada, whether out of love for his father or due to having seen the ugly side of bhaigiri in the lock-up, agreed. Since continuing in the college with a murder case to his name was next to impossible,

Jhingada started assisting his father in his plumbing work. He would spend his days accompanying the ageing man on his plumbing jobs and, in the evening, listening to lectures on how to deal with customers of various kinds.

Fate, however, had other plans for Munna Jhingada.

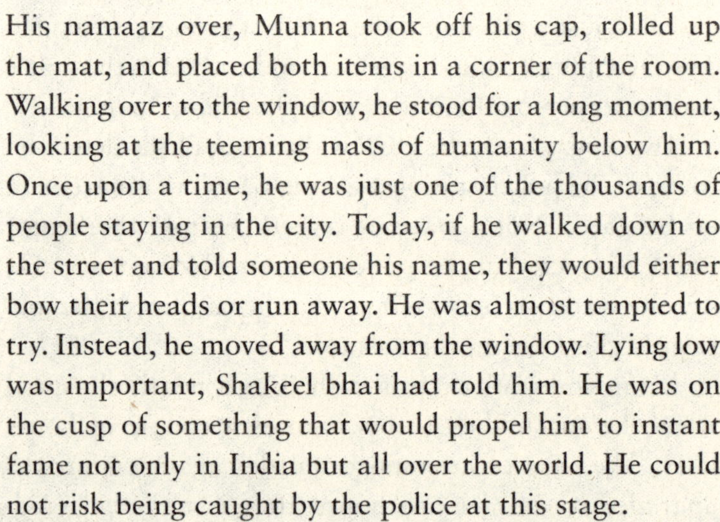

His namaaz over, Munna took off his cap, rolled up the mat, and placed both items in a corner of the room. Walking over to the window, he stood for a long moment, looking at the teeming mass of humanity below him. Once upon a time, he was just one of the thousands of people staying in the city. Today, if he walked down to the street and told someone his name, they would either bow their heads or run away. He was almost tempted to try. Instead, he moved away from the window. Lying low was important, Shakeel bhai had told him. He was on the cusp of something that would propel him to instant fame not only in India but all over the world. He could not risk being caught by the police at this stage.

Killer's Kindergarten

For the next three years, Jhingada led a quiet, uneventful life as a plumber's apprentice. As the months passed, people started putting the past behind them, and Jhingada and his family, who had become pariahs due to the murder case, slowly began to be accepted at social functions once again. It was then that Wazir's murder came back to bite Munna.

Wazir's bullying in college stemmed from the fact that his brother, Nasir, was a small-time thug in his locality. Nasir had been thirsting for revenge ever since Wazir's brutal killing at Jhingada's hands. One evening in March 1994, as Munna was on his way home after visiting a client, Nasir and some of his friends lay in wait for him. Over the last few weeks, Nasir had been discreetly seeking information on Munna's activities and schedule. After several weeks of reconnaissance and gathering information, Nasir finally laid a trap for Munna at a junction near his house which he was sure to pass no matter where he was coming from.

As Munna walked home, tallying up the day's accounts in his mind, Nasir blocked his path and told him that he was Wazir's brother. The mention of the name seemed to instantly wake up a sleeping demon inside Munna, who automatically went into attack mode.

Before Nasir and his group could make a move, Munna lunged at Nasir. However, this time, his enemies were well prepared. They had come armed with hockey sticks while Nasir had a chopper. They were all aware of Munna's fearless aggression, and started raining blows on him with their hockey sticks. Munna, however, fought back ferociously. In the ensuing melee, he managed to trip one of his assailants, snatched his hockey stick, and struck Nasir on the head repeatedly. The sight of their leader falling down bleeding unnerved the rest of the attackers. What little resolve they had left quickly melted away when a crowd started to gather.

Munna was arrested by the Meghwadi police, and

he readily confessed to having attacked Nasir in self-defence. Nasir, who had survived the attack, healed from his wounds by the time Munna came out on bail. Nasir's thirst for revenge had only intensified after his first scuffle with Munna, and he started looking for a second chance with renewed vigour.

The chance came around six months later, when he managed to corner Jhingada while he was having dinner with his friends in Vile Parle. He was, however, outnumbered, and had to run away after taking a severe beating from Munna and his friends. After three to four days of furious discussion, Jhingada and his friends surrendered to the Vile Parle police, and Munna was back in jail.

Around a year later, Nasir was found murdered in Jogeshwari and Munna, due to his past run-ins with him, became suspect number one. While it is still not clear whether it was Munna who killed Nasir, Munna was made a 'wanted accused' in the case. Munna made it clear to his father that he had no intention of going back to jail. His father then sent him to their native Uttar Pradesh, pleading with relatives to take care of him for a few months. In hindsight, it was a mistake.

Known as the Wild West of India, Uttar Pradesh is famous, or infamous, depending on how you look at it, for its country-made guns. People roam around freely with a *tamanchha,* local slang for a handgun, tucked in their waistbands, which are either crudely assembled in the scores of small manufacturing units in the state. A wedding is considered to be mild if *dunaalis,* or double-barrel rifles, are not fired in the air to celebrate the occasion.

It was only a matter of time before a couple of macho cousins brandished their tamanchhas and offered to teach Munna how to use one. Within a month of his coming to UP, target practice out in the fields with country-made revolvers became his favourite pastime. In the six months that he stayed in UP, Munna became skilled in the use of handguns and rifles.

In March 1997, Munna spoke to his father on the phone and they decided it was safe for him to return. Munna came back home quietly in the dead of night, and kept his head low for the next few days. However, a local informant—some suspect a henchman of Nasir's—saw him and tipped off an officer that he knew in the Oshiwara police station. The officer led a team to Munna's house, picked him up and handed him over to the Meghwadi police for interrogation in connection with Nasir's murder.

As Munna turned around, the door opened and a man walked in. Munna smiled.

'*Aao*, Rashid bhai,' he said. 'Is everything ready?'

'Yes,' the other man said. 'We leave for Pakistan tomorrow, *inshallah*.'

Bossman Beckons Belligerent Boy

Munna's arrest for Nasir's murder proved to be a major turning point for him. When around a month of interrogation by the toughest of cops did not elicit a confession from the hardened Jhingada, who was now a veteran with three stints in lock-up behind him, the police ran out of custody time and the court remanded him to judicial custody. He was sent to Arthur Road Central Jail, where he met Ismail Malabari. Ismail and his brother Rashid were high-ranking lieutenants in the D-gang hierarchy, and Ismail was in direct touch with Chhota Shakeel.

If there is one thing that a gang needs, and always gets, in abundant supply, it is foot soldiers. Fresh talent is always welcome for a criminal gang, as the more men it gets, the more crimes it can commit. The more crimes it commits, the more eyeballs it grabs, and the more feared it becomes.

One surefire recruiting ground for young talent is a central prison, where convicts and undertrials from all over the city are sent for crimes ranging from pickpocketing to murder. Gangland convicts, who quickly set up a system of communicating with their bosses from inside the jail by greasing the right palms, are spoilt for choice when it comes to recruiting in central jails. There is no dearth of people who turned to petty crime due to poverty and are willing to graduate to serious crimes if the money is good. Further, back in the '90s, just the chance of working for 'Dawood Bhai' was enough motivation for young criminals.

Ismail, one of Shakeel's top lieutenants, was impressed by Jhingada, who had refused to crack under intense police interrogation, and sought him out. In his first conversation with Ismail, an interview of sorts, Jhingada boasted of his hours of target practice. This, along with Jhingada's attitude, sealed the deal for him. Within a month, with Shakeel's help, Ismail arranged for bail for Jhingada.

On his last day in jail, Ismail gave Jhingada a bundle of cash and a phone number. '*Yeh* number *pe* phone *kar aur mera naam bol*,' Ismail told him. Jhingada sent half of the money to his parents, kept the rest for himself, and called the number he was given. He was directed to an address in Musafirkhana, where another D-gang enforcer was waiting for him. That same day, Jhingada spoke to Shakeel.

Shakeel told him that there was no dearth of money if he did the job right. Jhingada asked Shakeel to try him out, and that his actions would speak louder than his words. An amused Shakeel told him that he would be in touch.

A week later, Jhingada was taken to another small, nondescript room in Dongri, where Ismail's brother Rashid pulled a tarpaulin sheet off from over a table, revealing a large arsenal of imported arms and ammunition sent by Dawood from Pakistan, courtesy his friends in the Inter Services Intelligence (ISI), Pakistan's intelligence agency.

'Take your pick,' Rashid told him. 'Take enough for a team.'

Jhingada, overawed by the sight of the sophisticated weaponry, took his time before picking out two AK-56 assault rifles, two pistols and plenty of ammunition. He then asked Rashid who the target was. Rashid chuckled. 'Arun Gawli,' he said.

After establishing his base in Karachi with the ISI's help, Dawood had made it his mission to wipe out all other gangs in Mumbai so that he could rule the city all by himself. The two main obstacles in his path were Chhota Rajan and Arun Gawli. While Gawli had his own gang of diehard loyalists, a lot of Dawood henchmen recruited by Rajan shifted their loyalties when Rajan split with Dawood in 1993.

Jhingada and three other shooters set out the next day for Byculla, where Gawli was holding a rally to promote his political party, the Akhil Bharatiya Sena (ABS). During the entire rally, Jhingada and his team kept trying to get close enough to Gawli to shoot him. However, there was too large a crowd, too many guards around Gawli to deal with any threat, and too many policemen deployed at the rally, taking into account Gawli's criminal record.

Jhingada returned dejected, but Shakeel told him not to worry. It had been a test of guts, and Jhingada had passed. Shakeel then gave him his first real mission. He told Jhingada to gather as much information as he could about Gawli's aide Prakash Naik. Jhingada started hanging around the Dagdi Chawl and soon gave Shakeel a full report of Naik's movements.

A pleased Shakeel gave the go-ahead, and in August 1997, while Naik was exiting the Laxmi Industrial Estate after meeting a friend, Jhingada accosted him and emptied a pistol into his body.

It took the police around twenty-four hours to find out that the daring murder had been committed by the same young thin, diminutive-looking young man who had walked into the Jogeshwari police station six years earlier and calmly confessed to having stabbed his collegemate. Suddenly, Munna Jhingada was a person of interest. The Crime Branch asked for all information on Jhingada on a priority basis, and started building a dossier on him. Policemen who had interrogated him for the first time in 1991 were contacted, his house raided, and all his known friends picked up for questioning.

Jhingada's locality, too, was abuzz. Teenagers who were kids when he used to strut the lanes calling himself a bhai now idolized him. His association with the D-gang made him an instant hero in their eyes, while their parents prayed fervently to their god to save their own children from the path that their neighbour's son was walking.

In the midst of all this, Jhingada, hiding in a D-gang safe house, was smiling to himself and basking in the glory of the generous praise Shakeel had heaped on him. A lavish feast was held in his honour, and other D-gang members in Mumbai were now looking at him with respect rather than amusement.

Over the next three to four months, Munna Jhingada was like a weapon unleashed by the D-gang against its enemies. From August to October, he shot down no less than four aides of Gawli and Rajan in broad daylight, either with an AK-56 or with a Star pistol, to which he is said to have taken a liking to. His victims included financiers and enforcers for Rajan, and Jitendra Dabholkar, a close Gawli aide who was also senior member of the ABS. Jhingada teamed up with another small-time criminal, Sadiq Kalia, in killing a well-protected politician and founder of ABS, Dabholkar. The killing shook the city, demolished Gawli's political gameplan, and established the supremacy of Shakeel in the Mumbai gangland.

People who had once made fun of Jhingada learned to fear the mere mention of his name. The same neighbours who had once ostracized his family following his first arrest started cowering in terror when they saw Jhingada walking into the colony.

Guns became his sweetheart and his permanent companion. He was rarely without a pistol tucked under his shirt, and often carried an AK-56 in his car, adding all the more to his intimidating appearance.

The fear of police action was not a concern for him anymore. Nasir's murder had taught him that the police would come after him whether or not he was guilty, and he had lost his fear of third-degree torture long back. Besides, his employers, realizing his value, always kept him well hidden and constantly on the move.

Jhingada kept asking for more, and bigger jobs, and Shakeel kept telling him to be patient. However, his luck took a turn for the worse when the Santacruz police finally got a good tip and raided a house where he was staying in November 1997, cutting short his killing spree. The police found a large arsenal of assault rifles, pistols and live rounds in his house, and Jhingada ended up spending two months in custody of various police stations, and then close to two years in judicial custody. Central jail, again, was a cakewalk, as he was welcomed with open arms by the D-gang camp and hailed as a hero.

Meanwhile, in Dubai, Shakeel spared no effort in trying to get his latest favourite shooter back in action again. However, the amount of weaponry found in his house and the number of cases he was suspected to be involved in made this tough. Finally, in 1999, Jhingada managed to secure bail.

Like any smart gangster, Dawood and Shakeel realized that Jhingada had killed too many people too fast, and was attracting a lot of heat. The usual solution to the problem would have been to arrange a 'tip-off' to an encounter specialist and close the account forever. However, this time, Dawood had something else on his mind; something that he could use Jhingada for.

Bedlam in Bangkok

And so it was that Jhingada and Rashid Malabari were spending their last night in India in the small apartment tucked away in a corner of Pydhonie. They were poised to enter the annals of history.

Dawood had chosen them for a very special purpose. Ever since 1993, Dawood could not decide what he hated more: the fact that Rajan dared to defy him and start his own gang, or the fact that he had managed to portray himself as a patriotic don in the media, telling anyone who would listen that he had parted ways with Dawood because he had plotted against the country, thus winning himself a moral pedestal. Every time the word 'patriotic don' was used by the newspapers, or every time Rajan gave interviews to television news channels about his supposed patriotism, something burned inside Dawood with an intensity that was becoming unbearable with each passing day. He felt Rajan had simply run away like a rat to save his life, got into bed with the Indian intelligence services and was now going to town calling him a villain.

And this was where Munna Jhingada came in. When the time came and the gang cornered Rajan, he wanted someone who would be up for the job to assign the hit to. And Jhingada was the perfect candidate—a totally reckless, daredevil and dedicated hitman.

The next morning, Jhingada and Rashid flew to Pakistan with false passports, and were taken to Karachi, where they spent over a year close to Shakeel and Dawood.

And finally, in June 2000, Dawood's network of informants delivered what he had been screaming for. They gave him a definite lead on Rajan. Dawood immediately told Shakeel to start planning. Shakeel, who hated Rajan with an almost equal amount of intensity, lost no time in putting together a hit squad, and put Jhingada in charge.

Jhingada was overcome with gratitude when Shakeel told him the name of his next target. He promised Shakeel on everything he held sacred that he would get the job done or die trying.

In September 2000, Jhingada and his team were smuggled into Bangkok, where they spent ten days verifying their information about Rajan's whereabouts. It was confirmed that Rajan was staying in a flat in the Sukhumvit Soi area in Bangkok, with his trusted aide Rohit Verma, his wife and daughter.

On September 15 Jhingada's hit squad assembled around the corner from the nondescript apartment, where they removed their weapons from their bags, rechecked that they were working and loaded, and then ran to the flat. They entered the flat, headed straight to Rajan's room—where he had run to try and save himself—and opened fire. The door gave way under the hail of lead, and the killers moved in to be confronted by Verma.

Jhingada stepped forward and pumped thirty-two bullets into Verma's body before spraying the room with the remaining rounds in his gun. One round caught Verma's wife in the shoulder, but she survived. By sheer luck, Verma's daughter was out playing when Jhingada struck.

Rajan, too, sustained serious injuries in the attack, but Verma's loyalty gave him enough time to make good his escape. In spite of the fact that the main target had survived, Jhingada became an instant phenomenon.

The phones rang off their hooks across the world that day. Yes, they said across Asia, Chhota Rajan had survived a near fatal attack on his life. Yes, they confirmed in Mumbai, it was Munna Jhingada who led the attack.

The Mumbai police helplessly updated their dossier on Jhingada while getting a verbal lashing from the courts for letting him slip through their fingers. Jhingada was arrested shortly after by the Thai police and is currently in a Thai prison.

However, the Mumbai police are far from taking him into custody. The Pakistan government has also staked a claim to his custody, making assertions that he is, in fact, a Pakistani national named Mohammad Salim, and the two countries are currently locked in a diplomatic tussle over his extradition.

HITMAN 2

The Jettisoned Official Killer

Government's Gunmen

A large advertisement in a Dubai newspaper had announced the biggest event that the city was going to witness in a long time. Strangely, it was an India–Pakistan event that was being closely watched by intelligence agencies from across the world. Sleuths from Military Intelligence 6, or MI6, the UK intelligence arm, had taken position; Isreal's Mossad, India's Research and Analysis Wing (RAW) and Intelligence Bureau (IB) were also keeping a watchful eye as undercover agents. Pakistan's Inter-Services Intelligence (ISI) also spread its forces across the venue—the Grand Hyatt in Dubai.

Mr and Mrs Dawood Hassan Sheikh Ibrahim announce the wedding ceremony of their daughter Mahrukh to Junaid Miandad, son of Mr and Mrs Javed Miandad, Inshaallah, on 23 July 2005.

It was the walimah, a post-wedding feast organized by India's enemy number one Dawood Ibrahim, and Pakistani cricketer Javed Miandad, to celebrate their children's nuptial bond. On the one hand, fingers were being pointed at Miandad for his decision, and on the other, questions were being raised about how Dawood was able to do anything he wanted while India remained desperate to nab him. There was great curiosity around the lavish get-together—everyone wondered if Dawood would attend, and that too openly. But on the sidelines, a parallel plot was unfolding.

At the 24 Parganas in West Bengal, two men made their way into the Indian side of the border. Farid Tanasha and Vicky Malhotra—Chhota Rajan's most valued sharpshooters—had been absconding for a long time. They had been holed up in a south Asian country, and when Crime Branch sleuths first received a tip-off on their entry into India, they were puzzled. Why were they walking into a net, they wondered.

Meeran Borwankar, the then Crime Branch head, assigned Deputy Commissioner of Police Dhananjay Kamlakar to track Tanasha and Malhotra. The young officer got on the job without wasting any time. He tapped Tanasha's phone and was able to find out that he was visiting several destinations in the north of India. He and Malhotra were soon going to meet their handler in Delhi. But something was amiss—they were constantly in touch with India's IB for what seemed like a secret operation.

Tanasha's notoriety was established after the murder of Nepal's Member of Parliament Mirza Dilshad Beg, who was killed in Kathmandu in 1998. Tanasha was the main man behind the killing. And now he was being assigned a much bigger task. While DCP Kamlakar suspected that the duo had been told to eliminate a top businessman, the actual task was to kill Dawood Ibrahim at Dubai's Grand Hyatt when he attended his daughter's post-nuptial feast.

Unaware, Kamlakar and his team reached Delhi where the Indian intelligence agency's most daring operation was being plotted. Fake documents for Tanasha and Malhotra were ready and the duo was being briefed about the Grand Hyatt's floor plan, which would help them in getting their target and escaping. If all went well, Dawood—India's most wanted man—would breathe his last. And Chhota Rajan, who was baying for Dawood's blood, would heave a sigh of relief. Their prolonged rivalry had become intense after the attack on Chhota Rajan in Bangkok in September 2000 by Dawood's henchmen.

So far, Tanasha had made eight attempts to eliminate Dawood Ibrahim on the behest of his boss Rajan, but failed every time. In 1997, Tanasha and other Rajan gang members acquired Nepalese passports to facilitate their free movement in Pakistan.

In February 1997, Tanasha and Malhotra entered Karachi as cloth-sellers to carry out a recce of the area where Dawood lived—Sea Face, Defence Colony. Again, in March 1997, Tanasha travelled alone, rented a room at Al Mansoor Apartments in Defence Colony, and befriended a man named Junaid, who promised him weapons. A month later, Malhotra took with him seven men who were heavily armed. The group identified Dawood's house, but couldn't carry out the operation as Dawood's movements were extremely secretive.

Tanasha did not give up easily. Again, a few months later, he rented a place in Defence Colony. But once again Dawood's movements could not be tracked.

Two months later, when Dawood's daughter Maria died of malaria, Tanasha and his aides thought it would be a good time to attack as the don would be in mourning and could be caught off-guard. But the death kept Dawood confined to his house. The team went back to Nepal and returned again hoping to spot Dawood at the graveyard, but the don had been tipped off. Rajan then recalled them, fearing exposure.

The seventh attempt was made in October 1998. One of Rajan's hitmen, Nayan, was sent ahead as everyone knew Tanasha very well by then. Tanasha instructed Nayan to do all the groundwork, but told him that the shot at the don would be taken only by him. Nayan reached Karachi and rented a house close to Dawood's residence. He kept a watch on Dawood for fifteen days with the help of Junaid's network, but could not locate him.

The final attempt was in December 1998, when Nayan and Tanasha again entered Karachi and met Junaid and Ali Khan for arms. However, Dawood's spies found out about their presence in the city and averted the bid on his life.

These failed attempts were carried out without

extensive planning. The shooters did not think that reaching Dawood would be so difficult. They decided to give up on the plan till something concrete came up. Their opportunity came when the former IB chief Ajit Doval, hero of Operation Blue Star, hatched a plan to eliminate Dawood.

In an exclusive interview to the India Today Group, former home secretary and BJP MP R. K. Singh for the first time blew the lid off one of the most infamous chapters in India's effort to eliminate Dawood. According to him, the plot went haywire after the Mumbai Crime Branch stepped in, and Dawood too got a whiff of the plan and decided to skip the walimah.

At that time, it had become difficult for Dawood to move in and out of Pakistan as he had been designated as a globally-wanted terrorist by the United Nations. The walimah was the ideal opportunity for the Indian government to get rid of the don. However, the government did not want to be blamed for his death, so a decision was taken to engage members of the Chhota Rajan gang instead of sending commandos. It would then look like a gangwar, rather than a political move.

Doval took over as it was his pet project to get rid of Dawood. He got in touch with Rajan, who had split with Dawood after the Bombay blasts of 1993. Rajan needed two men who could be trusted with the job, and Tanasha seemed like the best choice. Tanasha was given the freedom to choose his own partner, and thus entered Vicky Malhotra, as both the shooters shared a good chemistry and were together even in the Mirza Dilshad Beg murder case.

Both men were trained at a secret location in India as the plan to eliminate Dawood was finalized. Getting Tanasha and Malhotra to Dubai was the IB's responsibility. Both were given fake travel documents and tickets to reach Dubai from Delhi.

One day, while Doval was in an animated conversation with Tanasha and Malhotra, DCP Kamlakar stormed into the room with his gun held out. Doval attempted to stop Kamlakar without letting out any of the information about the plot. A call was made to Kamlakar's boss Meeran Borwankar, but she too stuck to her guns. Kamlakar eventually left with Tanasha and Malhotra in his custody, not knowing that this smaller victory would actually be detrimental for the country in the bigger picture.

In any case, though, Dawood was a step ahead. He already had a whiff of the IB's plan and had made a decision to skip the daawate walimah. Though this operation didn't actualize, Tanasha gained. Being chosen to kill Dawood added an extra edge to his criminal résumé.

Deifying Don

When Farid Ahmed Tayyab Tanasha was sixteen-years-old, he often observed a young man selling movie tickets in black at the Sahakar Cinema in Chembur. Tanasha's family lived in the building opposite the theatre, and the ticket-seller's daring and swiftness fascinated him. The ticket-seller was Chhota Rajan, who was just starting off in the world of crime.

Gradually Rajan became the uncrowned king of Chembur. Tanasha's father noticed his son's admiration for Rajan and the underworld. He tried to make Tanasha understand the consequences of joining a gang, but it did not affect Tanasha. Whenever he got time and when his father was away for work, he would run to Sahakar Cinema and offer to help Rajan.

Rajan, too, became fond of this boy and often told him that one day he would become very big and powerful. One day Tanasha's father found out that his son had joined the gang and that his name would often crop up in petty crimes. The worried father went to meet Rajan and pleaded with him to stay away from his boy. Rajan politely told him that it was Tanasha who wanted to be with him, and he had not forced or called him to become a gang member.

As the meeting yielded no results, Tanasha's father decided to shift to a different locality so that the Rajan's menace in their life would end. He even got Tanasha a job in the Mazgaon docks so that he would remain occupied and not go back to Rajan. But Rajan was difficult to shake off. Every day, fancy cars would come to the docks to pick up Tanasha and then drop him in the evening. This irked the dock authorities and they sacked him within a month. Tanasha's father then shifted to a colony in Deonar. But even this failed to stop Rajan's influence over his son.

Tanasha was so keen to be with Rajan that he wanted to do something big for him to prove his loyalty. Tanasha soon got his opportunity. Rajan's guru, Bada Rajan, was killed by an auto-rickshaw driver named Chandrakant Safalika. In a daring act, dressed as a naval cadet with his gun hidden in the cavity of a thick book, Safalika followed Bada Rajan outside Esplanade Court when he was brought there for a hearing and shot him dead. Though he was arrested on the spot, Safalika managed to escape when he was being escorted to Thane jail. He then returned to his hideout in Chembur, unaware that Chhota Rajan's men were waiting for him. He was gunned down by Rajan's sharpshooter Danny.

As the police began a manhunt for Safalika's killer, Rajan expressed that he could not afford to lose Danny at that point of time. He wanted someone to take the blame. Tanasha jumped at this opportunity. He immediately offered to be the fall guy, and surrendered to the police. He knew what Bada Rajan meant to the gang, especially Chhota Rajan, and this gesture would only bring good things.

Rajan was very impressed with Tanasha and decided to get his cousin Sangeeta married to him so that he would always remain by his side. Tanasha's father did not approve of this match and placed a condition that the girl would have to convert to Islam. Sangeeta soon became Shehnaaz and got married to Tanasha.

Tanasha was now an integral part of the Rajan clan. He handled most of the gang's activities in Chembur; from extortion to real estate deals and killings, he was Rajan's right-hand and the most trusted lieutenant. He was everything for Rajan—a social worker, powerbroker, smuggler and hoodlum. More than this, he was a clever manipulator. He was now addressed as Farid bhai by the local residents.

In the early '80s, several gang members like Tanasha, Gungya, Sadhu Shetty alias Sadhu Anna, Bandya Mama, Danny alias Ganesh Devisingh Bisht, Anil Kashinath Mithbhavkar, Sanjay Raggad and others rose to power and were considered Rajan's army in Chembur. By the end of the decade, several cases of murder, rioting, attempt to murder, Arms Act under TADA were registered against them at different police stations in Mumbai.

Rajan had joined hands with Dawood Ibrahim, who was a well-known smuggler of gold and silver in the city, in the early'80s. In 1984, then Mumbai police commissioner Julio Ribeiro started turning the heat on Dawood, and he fled to Dubai. Rajan joined him. Dawood had handed over the reins of his operations in Mumbai to Rajan, who expanded Dawood's business not only in that city, but also across Nepal and Sri Lanka. The two most powerful members of the gang were not in city, and the reign of the underworld shifted to the hands of their punters, and Tanasha topped the list. Tanasha would be called to Dubai several times—one of the few gang members who had this privilege. He was treated like Rajan's son and would do anything for him.

Now a fearless gangster, Tanasha lived lavishly. He boasted about his closeness to Rajan at every moment. When Rajan split with Dawood over the serial bomb blasts in Mumbai, Tanasha remained loyal to Rajan. Dawood is said to have approached Tanasha and asked him to join hands with him. Tanasha, however, flatly refused the offer. By then, Rajan was in touch with the IB and RAW. He had become their tool against Dawood. Tanasha even used this to his advantage. He openly started boasting about his IB and RAW connections to everyone.

Once when he was summoned to the Tilak Nagar police station for some formalities following his release from jail on bail, a newly-appointed lady sub-inspector on probation asked Tanasha what his business was, as she was unaware that he was so powerful in the area. Tanasha, who enjoyed such moments, did not hesitate to tell her that he worked for an intelligence agency called RAW. Out of curiosity, she asked the same question again, and he politely responded by asking her a question. He asked her if she has seen a movie called *Kartoos*, starring Sanjay Dutt and Manisha Koirala. 'That film is based on my life,' Tanasha told the sub-inspector with a smirk. The officer found it amusing. Tanasha then went further, telling her that he was a celebrity among ganglords.

The Kathmandu Connection

Dilshad Mirza Beg was a prominent name in the D-Company. Mirza, as he was called by the company, had successfully established Dawood's network in Nepal. His entry into the company happened by chance. Both he and Dawood were struggling to set up their empires in Mumbai in the early '80s. At the time, Mirza also had links with Dawood's rivals. However, no one thought him to be of much importance till he reached Nepal and got in touch with the ISI.

As the surveillance along the Rajasthan and Punjab borders with Pakistan was very strict, Nepal became the easy conduit for drug lords to smuggle their goods. Mirza also found the porous Indo–Nepal border easy for him sneak between his home state of Uttar Pradesh and Nepal. Once he had set up a base in Nepal, where he felt safer, his notoriety grew so much that the Uttar Pradesh police announced a reward for his arrest. After the UP police failed to extradite Mirza from Nepal, the Interpol issued a red corner notice against his name.

After he rose to power, it was Dawood who asked for a collaboration, and Mirza agreed, realizing that he would be safer with Dawood. Dawood's reputation of transforming crooks into kings in India also helped him in Nepal. He joined politics, and playing the communal card in the election, Mirza won with a thumping majority. He was elected to the House of Representatives from the Terai district of Kapilvastu in 1994 and held ministerial portfolios in two governments. Three months before his death, he was the information and technology minister of Nepal.

According to the police, Mirza would take men from the D-Company to a safe location in Krishnanagar, which was his stronghold. Even during the blasts of '92–'93, it was Mirza who helped people like Salim Kutta, Feroz Wahid Zafar, Safdari and many more escape. Police also believed that Mirza regularly used his Krishnanagar mansion to shelter gangsters on the run from Indian enforcement agencies. His residence was also used for other illegal activities, including the confinement of abductees, drug-trafficking, gun-running and forging of documents. He was so effective that Dawood was able to establish a strong base in Kathmandu and even thought of shifting there for some time. Mirza's greed had turned him towards gun-running, smuggling arms procured from the Afghan Mujahedins and the ISI into India. Mirza was also the brain behind the bomb blast in Menka Talkies in Gorakhpur, UP in 1993.

Rajan knew that Mirza was the backbone of the D-Company in Nepal. Eliminating Mirza would be like attacking Dawood himself. This was an important assignment and had to be given to someone who was daring and fearless. He knew Tanasha was the right choice for this job. So Tanasha left with his five men and crossed the border into Nepal through Raxaul.

Rajan also contacted his other sharpshooter, Rohit Verma, who was already in Nepal, and asked him to organize the killing with Tanasha, but advised him not to strike in Kathmandu. A shooter organized by Babloo Srivastava, a Delhi based ganglord who specialized in kidnapping, also helped in the mission, as he had scores to settle with Mirza. Mirza had helped him get a Nepali passport but later abandoned him when he was arrested in Singapore. Babloo thought that Mirza had done this deliberately on orders from Dawood and wanted revenge. He contacted his aide in Nepal and gave him some money to arrange for a safe house in Kathmandu. However, despite taking the money, they were unable to find a place.

Tanasha, meanwhile, stayed in a village close to Krishnanagar and started keeping a watch on Mirza. Over the next few days he found out that Mirza had two wives and would shuttle between their two homes. On 29 June 1998, around 9.30 in the evening, Mirza left his safe hideout and went to meet his second wife in Siphal in the Chabahil area. Tanasha and his men had already positioned themselves around the place where Mirza would stop his car. As soon as he got down, a volley of bullets began flying from all directions. Mirza was caught by surprise and did not have the time to defend himself. Tanasha and his men pumped seven bullets into his body, after which he collapsed to the ground and died.

All five men fled from the spot and dispersed as was planned. While Verma and the other cronies managed to get out of Nepal, Tanasha was stuck in the Himalayan kingdom. He had arranged for a passport and ticket but all his documents were with Verma, and there was no way he could establish contact with him as the Nepal government was on the lookout for the MP's killers.

Tanasha decided to take refuge in a small village on the outskirts of Nepal. He thought it would be good to hide there for few days till he found a way to escape. There he met a girl who took a liking to him. Her name was Reshma, and she was a resident of the village. He told her that he had come to Nepal for a job and had lost his documents. There was no way he could return to India. Reshma decided to help him out. She knew a few agents who made fake documents and introduced

Tanasha as her husband. They both made documents with fake names and addresses. On the day that Tanasha was supposed to leave Nepal and fly to Delhi, he confessed to Reshma that he had killed Mirza. He also confessed his love for her. Reshma agreed to move to India with him.

Both left for Delhi and got married a few days later. Reshma had relatives in Delhi and they resided with them for a few days before Tanasha took her back to Chembur.

Interestingly, suspicions have been raised as to the way Reshma met Tanasha, came to India with him, and then vanished again after he was gunned down by Bharat Nepali's men. Tanasha and Reshma have a daughter and the girl is being taken care of by his first wife Shehnaaz. Reshma abandoned the child in a boarding school and disappeared mysteriously.

The Last Wish

Being on a mission to kill Dawood for most of the time he spent in the underworld made Tanasha a lucrative target. Also, for Dawood, killing Tanasha meant getting rid of Rajan's right-hand man.

It was 3 June 2010. Tanasha had a deep urge to see his three-year-old daughter. His wife Reshma had called him over the phone and told him that the girl had been crying all evening. Not a minute had she slept or kept quiet. Tanasha promised to get home soon.

Around 9 o'clock in the evening he came home looking tense. He first went to his daughter, picked her up and hugged her. She seemed to be at ease and soon started playing with her father. He told Reshma that his legs were hurting. She offered him dinner and a foot massage later. There was an uncanny silence outside Tanasha's ground floor flat in the Meghana Cooperative Housing Society. He had seven dogs in his compound, but surprisingly none was barking. His ten bodyguards, who were always playing cards and strolling outside the society, were not around. A few had taken leave while the others were just missing. According to Reshma's statement to the police, five bodyguards were supposed to be there in his compound. It turned out they had taken the dogs for a walk.

Around 9.45, Tanasha retired to his bedroom and his wife Reshma began massaging his feet. His daughter was in his lap, playing. When Reshma finished massaging his feet, she went to the kitchen, leaving Tanasha and the toddler in the bedroom. All was quiet inside but there were movements outside his house. Five men had entered the society compound. They knew that the usual hustle-bustle of Tanasha's bodyguards was missing that day. The coast was clear. The sprawling flat had two entrances—front and rear. Three men decided to wait outside in case someone came to help him out. The other two pushed open the rear entrance and barged inside.

They went through the kitchen and entered the bedroom where their target was present. As the men entered the room, Tanasha tried to retrieve his revolver, which he kept under his pillow. But the assailants began firing at him. A bullet hit him on the side of his chest.

He was injured but he knew that the men might hit his daughter. So he asked them to wait and put his daughter aside. He raised his hands in surrender and smiled at his killers, pleading that his daughter should not be hurt. The assailants pumped five bullets into him. Hearing the gunshots, Reshma ran into the bedroom, only to see her husband lying in a pool of blood. The killers looked at her and left the room. Three bullets had entered his skull and two had hit him in the chest. He died on the spot.

According to the police, six to eight people were involved but only two entered the house. The building guard, who was normally at the front entrance, was at the rear gate that night. Both doors to Tanasha's flat were open when the assailants walked in. It was obvious that it would not have been possible to get into Tanasha's house unhindered without the involvement of a close confidante.

Tanasha's death was a big blow to Rajan. Apart from the fact that he was considered the main lieutenant in the Chembur area, all Rajan's financial work was done through Tanasha, as he had been loyal to the don since his childhood days. While it was clear to some that this killing was the handiwork of an enemy of Rajan's, some people suspected that it was Rajan himself who was behind this murder. The two men had been having some differences related to real estate investment issues, and Tanasha was planning to quit the gang. The mere thought of Rajan bumping off his trusted aide created a flutter in his own gang. Rajan had to call his men himself to assure them that Tanasha was like his son and that he would never do this to him.

Two days after Tanasha was murdered, the Mumbai Crime Branch received leads that the shootout was carried out by professional sharpshooters hired from inside a jail in the state. Small-time gangster Bharat Nepali, a sworn enemy of Rajan's, then claimed responsibility for the attack. To avoid suspicion, he said he hired shooters from other gangs who were in jail and did not use his own men.

Sources said Nepali used his men only for reconnaissance and vigilance when Tanasha was visiting Ajmer. Nepali had another advantage which helped him carry out the murder of Tanasha so easily. He had worked with him earlier when he was in Rajan's gang as well. Tanasha's habits, his style of working, his contacts and every other minute detail was known to Nepali. Perhaps that was the reason why he chose his friend as a target. To kill a gangster like Tanasha in his own bedroom with such precision and ease was a huge victory for him in the underworld. And Nepali, after his break from Rajan, had been itching to establish himself as a powerful boss. He had used all his financial power to prove the same. He had made money through years of trade in narcotics, and could therefore hire the best shooters to execute his plan.

There was another reason why he chose Tanasha as a target. According to police sources, Tanasha was gaining an edge in the collection of extortion money. Even a gangster like Chhota Shakeel was troubled by this, and there were suspicions that he gave Nepali and Santosh Shetty the contract to eliminate Tanasha.

Both Nepali and Shetty had been close lieutenants of Rajan—they were the ones who smuggled Rajan out of a hospital in Bangkok in 2000 after he was shot at by Dawood's gang. But both broke from Rajan and formed their own outfits, vowing to do away with the Rajan gang. Nepali was an ace shooter who could rope in criminals from UP for contract killings, and Shetty was a top-rung drug smuggler who had vast contacts with the underworld in South-East Asia, South Africa and Europe. He functioned as the cerebral part of the axis.

Apparently, apart from real estate matters, Tanasha had been eyeing the protection money racket, estimated to be around Rs 3,000 crore. Many old buildings in the neighbourhood of Nagpada and around were being redeveloped, and the main source of protection money came from builders who would pay the underworld to threaten residents of the buildings to get them to move out.

Nepali knew that Tanasha was trying to grab a lion's share of these earnings. Already he controlled the *hafta* from developers in Chembur, which was his stronghold—no other gang was allowed to enter the area. The problem started when Tanasha began eyeing Nagpada, Dawood's stronghold. He had also crossed swords with a relative of Dawood Ibrahim from the Bohri Mohalla area, over sharing of the money. The fight had escalated to such a level that Tanasha had threatened to kill him.

Apart from all this, Tanasha had also incurred the D-Company's wrath by planning numerous attacks to bump off the don in Karachi.

In fact, the police had received information that a trusted aide of the don was planning an attack on Rajan. Even Rajan was aware of this. Understanding the gravity of the situation, Rajan had told Tanasha to leave Mumbai till the matter died down. But Tanasha was overconfident. He was under the impression that no one could get past his security. However, though he knew that it would be difficult for anyone to kill him in Chembur, he had taken some extra precautions. He had increased his security cover from five to ten guards a few months before the attack on him.

For residents, the shooting of 'Farid bhai' was an unpleasant rewind to the first time something like this had happened in the early '90s. The Bada Rajan faction had gunned down a fellow-gangster and black-marketer in cinema tickets outside Sahakar Cinema.

Tanasha's funeral was attended by many Rajan men as well as the wife of Chhota Rajan, the current Shiv Sena corporator Rajiv Chaugule alias Raja Bhau, and small-time Marathi actors and film producers, including a prominent film producer in Bollywood, Romesh Sharma.

Amidst the fanfare during his last journey, one could forget that the deceased was a brutal man, feared in the colony, and responsible for killing many.

HITMAN 3

Blood Guzzling Bagga

Mujhe Khoon Chahiyye

The cops were frustrated. They had never met a criminal who did not break down after being given the third-degree. This was the hardest nut to crack.

Suddenly a constable came running. 'Saab, he says to give him a bottle of his favourite drink and he will start answering all our questions.'

The officer lost his cool and exploded. *'Doka firla aahe ka tujha, kai ekaila yet nahi?'* (Have you gone mad or you have gone deaf?)

'Why sir?' the constable asked.

'How can we give him alcohol in the lock-up—?'

The constable cut in before the officer could complete his sentence.

'Saab, he does not want alcohol, he wants a bottle of blood.'

Venkatesh Bagga Reddy, alias Baba Reddy, the self-proclaimed Kali devotee, did not break despite undergoing the notorious third degree. But he began singing like a canary when the cops managed to procure the blood of a slaughtered goat from a nearby slaughterhouse and offered it to him in a bottle. After this, Bagga was only too happy to provide all the answers that the police needed from him.

At the young age of twenty-eight, Bagga was the most mysterious character in the history of Mumbai's underworld. According to Hindu mythology, there was a demon Raktabeeja's who was given a boon—every drop of blood of his that fell on the ground would create one more demon. The only way he could be defeated was to ensure that his blood did not spill. When Kali fought with him, she ensured that his blood did not fall by stretching her tongue and licking up each drop of blood pouring from the demon. Bagga believed in this myth, and thought that blood would give him life and drinking the blood of 'demons'—in this case, his enemies—would make him stronger.

This Kali *bhakt* was a lethal-killing machine who would mix rice with the blood of his victims and savour the dish. Raw meat and blood was his staple. On those days when he could not get human blood, he would drink animal blood. And when animal blood could not be had, Bagga would cut himself and add his blood to the plate to enjoy his meals.

Another thing that set Bagga apart fom other members of the underworld, was that he would accept only non-Hindu targets. And he always remained blatant about his communal preferences.

Originally from Mushirabad, the commercial centre

of Hyderabad in Andhra Pradesh, Bagga had dropped out of school after Class IX. He took a course at the Industrial Training Institute (ITI) in his hometown and then began worked as a welding engineer in a small firm. On the side, Bagga continued to pursue his passion for body-building. He loved to show off his muscles, and pumping iron gave him great satisfaction. Later, when Bagga was working in a garage, a person known as Haji bhai offered him a job as his bodyguard. Bagga agreed instantly, but there was only one hitch. He would have to shift to Bombay. After much deliberation, Bagga decided to take up the offer, knowing that Bombay would give him more power and money.

In the year 1989, Bagga moved to Mulund, a central suburb in Bombay, where he also began working as a bouncer in a bar. Soon, the hefty man began hobnobbing with businessmen and underworld criminals who were regulars at the bar. It was his peculiar middle name that everyone identified him by—Bagga.

Bodybuilder Bagga

Bagga picked up the most important trait in the underworld: passing on information from one person to another, one gang to another. This not only earned him extra money but also a reputation for having contacts with the underworld. His first brush with crime took place after he met Dimple Dada in a bar in Chembur. Dimple Dada felt that Bagga had the potential to be part of his gang. Moreover, he had a physique that was intimidating enough to throw some weight around. So he offered him a place in his gang at a handsome monthly salary. Bagga could not resist the offer and he joined the gang with the first assignment already at hand. He was asked to kidnap an industrialist's son from a school in Bandra. He was promised one lakh rupees for the task, a huge amount at the time.

An excited Bagga meticulously planned the kidnapping. He studied his target's daily movements and closely observed the school premises. On the day he executed the plan, Bagga kept a watch on the child from his house. As soon as his father dropped him off at the school, Bagga began walking towards the boy. Just then he spotted two policemen in the vicinity and that got him worried. However, he fearlessly picked up the boy and put him in a Maruti van. The cops began chasing him as also the private guards meant to protect the child.

Bagga decided to abandon the child and escape. But the fear of ridicule and derision at chickening out forced him to return to his hometown in Andhra Pradesh and go into hiding for a while. In any case, since the police were hot on his heels, he felt it would be wiser to disappear from the scene.

When communal riots broke out after the demolition of Babri Masjid, Bagga returned to Mumbai with an agenda. He wielded a sword and began a stabbing spree in the western suburbs whenever he found a Muslim alone on the streets. Bagga later explained to the police that he believed that he was avenging the death of Hindus. This was also the time when he first became aware of his liking for blood. He killed several people from the Muslim community, every time tasting their blood. The police picked him up among many others but he showed no remorse.

In jail, the inmates refused to stay in the same cell as Bagga. They feared that he would hurt them because of his thirst for blood.

Soon Bagga was released from jail and his fear of committing crimes disappeared. He decided to use his newfound courage to find a footing in the underworld once again. He started working at a bar in Mulund, a job he knew best which also helped him to network. Every day, he would flex his muscles to shoo away the problem-makers and beat up those who created a ruckus or refused to pay up.

Simultaneously, he also worked as a bodyguard of Gurunath Koth, a Shiv Sena trade union leader. He later moved on to become the bodyguard of Dhananjaya Shetty, owner of the famous Chandni Bar.

In the process, Bagga was exposed to several gangsters, including Sanjay Ghati and Viju Shetty of the Chhota Rajan gang. They were impressed by this man who could single-handedly beat up a dozen men like him. Soon they introduced Bagga to their boss and got him enrolled in the Rajan gang. Rajan was impressed with Bagga's record of communal killings during the riots and put him on special assignment to kill Dawood Ibrahim's men involved in the serial blasts in Mumbai.

Soon Bagga became the highest-paid contract killer, commanding the most coveted perks in gangland. He was paid thirty thousand to fifty thousand rupees per job. He also made extra money through extortions.

Despite being a killing machine, Bagga was a regular at temples and shrines in the city. One such visit to the Sitladevi temple in Mahim turned Bagga's life around. He saw a woman and instantly took a liking for her. It was love at first sight. Bagga talked about it later in quite a filmy manner. Apparently the woman was sitting on a platform, deep in her thoughts. Bagga, without realizing it, stood staring at her, without blinking his eyes even once. When the woman noticed him, she stood up and began walking away briskly. Bagga followed her and saw her entering the lane near the Makhdoom Shah Baba dargah.

Poison of Love

Being as prejudiced as he was, Bagga did not want to enter a Muslim area. He found himself in a quandary. His feet did not want to move, but his heart was forcing him forward. Bagga was so attracted to the woman that he could not stop himself. He began investigating everything there was to know about the girl: who she was, what she did. He began visiting the area every day and followed the girl while she offered flowers to the shrine.

Bagga learnt that the woman's name was Shehnaz. She was a Muslim, which shattered Bagga. But, as they say, love is the biggest leveller and breaks all barriers. Bagga decided to propose marriage to her. He casually struck up a friendship with her and began wooing the woman. Shehnaz also felt attracted towards Bagga. But before saying yes to the marriage proposal, she placed one condition. Bagga would have to convert to Islam.

Unimaginable before he met her. But now, a fanatic Muslim-hater like Bagga was so besotted with Shehnaz that he agreed to the conversion. Venkatesh Bagga Reddy became a Muslim and renamed himself as Aziz Reddy.

With marriage, Bagga's brutalilty began diminishing. Before, according to his own confessions, Bagga had killed thirteen Muslims, but after he met Shehnaz, he decided to turn a new leaf. This also made him lower his guard as a killer and his levels of alertness slackened. And, as a maxim goes in the underworld: '*Jiski nazar* game *se hati, woh* game *se hata*' (The one who loses focus in the game, loses the game).

On 26 July 1998, the Special Operations Squad (SOS) of the Mumbai Crime Branch received a tip-off about Bagga. The Mumbai police were hot on his trail and had not been able to lay their hands on him for a long time. When one of Bagga's close aides squealed on him, his whereabouts and criminal history, the cops decided to get him come what may.

For the six men armed with AK-47 assault rifles, it was a do or die situation. Either they could bring down the notorious Venkatesh Bagga Reddy, or succumb to certain death at his hands. After all, Bagga was nowhere close to the other criminals they had dealt with. The dossiers of the Mumbai police had never had such a bloodthirsty criminal, literally.

The squad circled a decrepit building where they suspected Bagga had taken shelter with five others. One after the other, they marched upstairs and barged into a tiny room, catching the suspects unaware. Knowing well that they were in no position to counterattack, the five men in the room surrendered in no time.

But Bagga was not one to budge. Confidence in his own physical strength had intoxicated him. He pounced on the squad without any fear of being shot. The cops, however, had luck on their side. They overpowered him and handcuffed him to limit his movements. They had been clearly instructed to arrest and not to kill. They also seized arms and ammunition from him.

Bagga's arrest was big feather in the cap of ACP Pradeep Sawant. Bagga was lodged in Arthur Road jail for a year. Bagga could not believe that he had been arrested so easily. But he kept making plans while he was in custody. He decided that once he was out of the jail he would not fall into the hands of the police again.

Bagga Begins the B-Gang

After his release on bail, Bagga made a fake passport and escaped to Malaysia, where he met Chota Rajan. Here, with the help of Rajan, he got a fake passport in the name of Michael Fernando and visited Indonesia. Rajan had decided to use him in his drug business. He was given charge of the working of a mandrax-manufacturing unit in Bathan.

As Bagga realized how lucrative the drug trade

business was, he began to take an interest in the deals and made friends with Rajan's left-hand man, Santosh Shetty. Both Shetty and Bagga connected instantly and became good friends. The other gang members envied them and started complaining to Rajan about them. Allegations of the misappropriation of funds reached Rajan, who soon began to doubt Bagga. This led to a clash of interest between Bagga and Rajan, and soon differences began to grow. Later, Bagga and his friend Santosh Shetty set up a hotel, Indian Mantra, in Jakarta, in which they invested about twenty crore rupees.

Bagga flew back to India in December 2002. He was aware that the number of his enemies was increasing. He knew Dawood's men were looking for him in Mumbai, so he decided to change base and to Kashi in Uttar Pradesh. During his time in Kashi, he got in touch with Kishore Garikapatti, a close aide of former Dawood man Subash Thakur. Kishore offered him shelter and money if he worked for them. Bagga did not have much of an option—he needed the support.

Bagga was given the job of killing people who were against Thakur. Bagga and Thakur had enemies from the Rajan group in common.

In a daring incident, Bagga shot down Narendra and Bavendra, two gunmen who had killed actress Manisha Koirala's secretary, Ajit Dewani. This became his biggest hit. Happy with his successful series of killings in Uttar Pradesh, Thakur asked him to move back to Mumbai as he had some scores to settle with Rajan's men. Bagga did not want to return to the city, so he decided to go back to Hyderabad and set up base there. After reaching Hyderabad, he set up the B-Company, as he had also earned the name Baba Reddy. In fact, he operated under six different names.

By now, Bagga was involved in twenty-one cases in Hyderabad, Mumbai and UP. In Hyderabad, his career chart progressed rapidly. He became a weapon supplier, importing weapons from a dealer in Indonesia and supplying them to other gangs. He imported twenty weapons for his own personal use as well. He also extorted money from businessmen in Hyderabad. He allegedly extorted five to ten lakh rupees from Suresh Agarwal and one Raju, both well-known cricket bookies. He also extorted seven lakh rupees from the proprietor of the Golconda Cigarette Factory. Meanwhile, he continued to pay attention to his drug factory in Jakarta.

When he formed his new gang his old friends came to help him out and became an integral part of the mafia in Hyderabad. Rajesh Madrasi, Anand Prem, Bala, Mental Sanjay, Prem alias Pandit and Nilesh alias Shailesh became his trusted advisors and gang members, while his old friends Asif and Chapala Srinu were entrusted with the task of settling financial and land disputes. The police said that Bagga used to settle land disputes and extort money from realtors, businessmen and film personalities. He was involved in several kidnappings for ransom.

Bagga was known to spend lavishly. He owned forty acres of land in his native Nalgonda district. He also had investments in Bangkok, Malaysia and Singapore. He is said to have thirty-eight bank accounts across the world.

Though a gangster, Bagga was different from others. While other gangsters demanded extortion money in cash, Bagga always insisted on cheque payments. Bagga had a full-time chartered accountant who managed all his transactions. He also had connections in the police force and the political system in Hyderabad.

In 2005, the police seized five foreign-made sophisticated firearms, including an Israel-made Uzi sub-machine gun, three 9-mm pistols and a huge quantity of ammunition from Bagga's men in the city's posh Banjara Hills. When the police asked his men to surrender, they opened fired on them. The police finally managed to arrest five men. The police invoked the Andhra Pradesh Control of Organised Crime Act against Bagga and his associates, who were charged with carrying out illegal activities in Hyderabad. However, Reddy and his men were acquitted of the charges as all the witnesses turned hostile and there was not enough evidence.

Within a year, Reddy was free. He returned to Hyderabadfrom Thailand in December 2007 and resumed his extortion and land settlement activities.

On 30 April 2008, film producer Nikhil Reddy received a phone call on his office landline. The call was from Aziz Reddy asking him to cough up protection money or face consequences. Nikhil immediately informed the Banjara Hill police asking for protection. This extortion bid turned out to be the last one for Bagga.

Bodybag

In May the same year, the police received a tip off that Bagga and his associates were to visit Banjara Hills. This time the cops decided to eliminate him permanently as he had made a mockery of the system many times. Encounters had become a rage in Mumbai, and the Hyderabad police were not far behind. In the afternoon, a group of ten Task Force commandos split themselves in two groups and took their position in the area where Bagga was supposed to arrive. He had an appointment with a landlord to settle a property dispute and also to extort money from him. Though the commandos had started a search in the area, they did not know the exact location of the gangster's meeting place as he was known to change venues at the last moment.

The roads were cleared and no other vehicle was allowed to come that side. The search continued for over two hours till, finally, a vehicle which they suspected was carrying their quarry approached and was let through. The Task Force personnel saw three men alighting from a vehicle. The cops waited till all the three men were out of the car. One of the three was identified as Bagga.

As the policemen closed in on the gang, Reddy and his associates sensed that they had been surrounded and tried to flee. The police asked them to surrender, but Bagga started firing at the police. The gangsters chose three corners and hid themselves. The exchange of fire continued for an hour. It is said that Bagga's two associates managed to flee from the spot but Bagga was killed. It took ten men to gun down one man. Despite being hit by a bullet in his right arm, he continued to fire. In the end, the commandos were able to surround him and fired at him indiscriminately. He died on the spot.

It later turned out that it was one of Bagga's close associates who tipped off the police. The associate wanted to topple him and take over the gang. But the cops ensured that the gang disintegrated after Bagga's death.

Shahnaz, too, could never be traced.

HITMAN 4
The Maya of Mobsters

Mahindra Makes a Mark in the Mob World

Remember Vivek Oberoi from *Shootout at Lokhandwala*? The spunky, crazy, unpredictable, volatile gangster he portrayed on the screen was quite close to an actual hitman, Maya Dolas.

Everyone who knew Maya Dolas agrees that, before August 1991, there was hardly anyone who had heard his name. The same people also agree that, after August 1991, there was hardly anyone in the city who hadn't.

Born Mahendra Dolas in 1966 in Sion, Dolas was among the scores of young, unemployed youth who joined the underworld for the sake of money as well as respect. Maya began his career in crime by working as a henchman for the Arun Gawli gang in 1988 but was soon recruited by Chhota Rajan, who was at the time still with Dawood Ibrahim Kaskar and his chief recruiter and enforcer.

An old-time member of the gang recalls Dolas as one of the many young toughs employed by the gang back then, who were managed by Appa Jadhav, a mid-level D-Company enforcer. 'A lot of builders close to the D-gang were provided henchmen as security against attacks by other gangs. Maya used to be among the young boys who would hang around the offices or construction sites of builders close to the gang when he started, and reported directly to Jadhav. The job was more about looking tough than doing anything else. Later, he started going out on firing jobs, but was still one among many. He hardly had any standing of his own,' he recalls.

Maya's first brush with fame came when he participated in the murder of Ashok Joshi in December 1988, along with Sunil Sawant, one of the D-gang's main shooters, and several others.

Joshi was the undisputed lord of Kanjurmarg at the time. Dawood was on a mission to eliminate all local gangs so he could claim the city for himself, and Joshi was among the local ganglords who were standing in the way of Dawood's dream.

Joshi was also exceedingly cautious. He kept changing his location every couple of days, travelled in a convoy of two to three cars, and always decided the route to his destination at the last minute. Dawood's men knew that they would have to put in some special effort to crack this one. Finally, they hit upon an age-old solution.

'It has been a favourite tactic of war, right from the times of kings, to rely on the betrayal of people to topple their superiors. All that one needs to do is to find the right person and the right motivation. In this case, the right person was Joshi's driver, and the motivation was to work for "Dawood bhai" once the job was done. Falling for the promises, Joshi's driver agreed to relay his employer's plans so that an ambush could be set up,' retired assistant commissioner of police (ACP), Jaywant Hargude, recalls.

As soon as Joshi decided to shift to Pune from Kanjurmarg, his driver informed Sawant, who mobilized a large team of men armed to the teeth. The team of six men lay in wait in a Maruti car near Khopoli, which falls on the way for anyone heading from Mumbai to Pune.

Joshi's driver, who was at the wheel, was extra tense. He had described to Rajan the car he would be driving in. Rajan had in return told him that he would at some point overtake his car and block his path, which would be his signal to get out.

Joshi's driver kept his eyes peeled and peered intently at every vehicle that passed by to see if it was going to overtake them. His 'signal' did come, but it was followed by his death. Sawant's van, which had been following Joshi's car ever since it entered Khopoli, did overtake the car, but Sawant and his men started firing before the van came to a halt. Joshi's driver took bullets in his entire body, and car swerved out of control. Sawant's team then stepped out of the van and riddled the car with more than one hundred and eighty rounds from automatic rifles. It is said that the shooters did not even stop to peer inside the car to check whether all the four occupants, including Joshi, were dead; they just got back into the van and sped away.

The plan had never included recruiting the driver; he was always slated to die. A man who could betray one employer could just as easily betray his next one.

As audacious as the murder was, it did little to increase Maya's standing in the gang. Even at that time, he was just one of the many shooters working for Dawood who had participated in a big crime.

That changed in August 1991, when Dolas was arrested in connection with one of the scores of firing cases registered against the D-Company in the early '90s. A few days later, while he was being taken to the Mazagaon court to be produced before the magistrate, Maya did what few had the guts to do at the time.

As he was being walked into the court premises, Maya slipped a hand in his pocket and removed powdered chilli that he had been hiding. Turning to one of his police escorts, he threw the powder in his eyes. As the stunned and disoriented policeman dropped to the ground screaming, trying to tear his burning eyes out of their sockets, Maya turned towards the other constable, who was trying to decide whether to attack Maya or go to his colleague's aid.

The split-second hesitation proved to be unfortunate for the second constable, as Maya had already fished out a blade from somewhere in his clothes. He slashed at the constable several times, drawing blood, and ran out of the court premises, leaving both policemen lying on the ground in agony.

His actions in the court compound on that day were among the many that would cement his reputation as a fearsome gangster. The khaki uniform carried a lot of respect in those days, and people were hesitant to resist arrest or even argue with a uniformed policeman. For an arrested accused to attack policemen, inside a court premises no less, and escape, was unheard of. People did escape from custody in those days, but by giving policemen the slip, taking advantage of their laxity or by using a diversion. Actually attacking a cop was something that few would have dared to do.

Old-timers in the police force still wonder how Maya managed to procure a blade and powdered chilli and smuggle them to the court on his person. Some say he did it with the help of his lawyer, others suspect he greased some palms while inside the lock-up, while some also theorize that his friends slipped him the chilli and the blade during an earlier court appearance. As Dolas did not walk away alive the next time he came face-to-face with policemen, this is a question the police still try to guess an answer for.

However he managed to do it, Dolas established an image in the eyes of the people that he was not only daring but also resourceful enough to be able to get what he wanted in spite of being behind bars.

Mahindra's Transformation into Maya

The next turning point in Dolas' career came less than a week after his escape, when he was tasked with eliminating three of the surviving members of the Ashok Joshi gang.

Dolas and his friends lay in wait for their targets on a busy street in Kanjurmarg. Dolas has chosen the venue and setting of the hit job, and this, too, worked towards building his fearsome image.

Armed with AK-47s, Dolas and his friends stood patiently by the side of the road till their targets approached. The three unfortunate gang members, however, were not by themselves. They were part of a Ganpati immersion procession organized by the Ashok Joshi gang. Other hitmen might have been deterred by the fact that there were too many people present and cancelled the job at that moment. Not Maya Dolas.

The hit squad stood calmly by the side of the road till the procession was close enough. Then Dolas stepped forward and stood in the middle of the road, AK-47 in hand.

Calling out the names of his targets, accompanied by abusive words, Dolas opened fire and his friends followed suit. All the three men were cut down in the hail of automatic fire even as the crowd around them ran helter-skelter, screaming and tripping over each other. Five innocent bystanders were killed and eight injured.

Neither the presence of the large number of potential eyewitnesses, nor the fact that Ganesh *utsav* always has a heavy police *bandobast* acted as a deterrent. This was also the first time that AK-47s were used for a hit job in a city used to witnessing gangland killings by pistols and swords.

The audacity and the brutal nature of the murders made Dolas the subject of conversation among people throughout the city, policeman and civilian alike. While the cops started taking a close interest in this upstart who had so arrogantly defied them by committing a multiple homicide in full public view using imported automatic assault rifles, the common man started worrying for his own safety.

Overnight, loyalties that earlier lay with other gangs shifted to Dawood, taking him one step further towards realizing his dream of ruling the city. Phones rang off the hook over the next few days, with businessmen who earlier paid protection money to other gangs being reminded of the daring murder, accompanied by a not-at-all subtle threat that they would meet the same fate if they did not fall in line.

While Maya's escape from court told people he was not afraid of the police, the Kanjurmarg shootout gave out the message that eyewitnesses were not a problem for him either. In other words, no one was safe from Maya Dolas.

As with a lot of stories, the story of the shootout gathered meat in the telling and, somehow, Dolas' jailbreak was linked to the shootout. It did not take long for people to assume that Dolas was broken out of jail by 'bhai' specifically for this '*bada kaam*' or important task. Being assigned a bada kaam was an honour for henchmen in those days, and being broken out of jail to be assigned one meant the boss trusted you enough to go to that extent for you. It took people even less time to theorize that Dolas was one of the boss' *khaas* or special henchmen specifically handpicked for the job, and with this theory, Dolas earned tremendous respect, and more importantly, fear of the people overnight.

Within a week, Maya had gone from being just another shooter to a fearsome, daring and reckless killer who would come after you if you crossed Dawood.

The D-gang top brass, who knew that being feared was far more advantageous than being loved, was quick to capitalize on Dolas' newfound image. He was assigned job after job for maximum visibility, and Dilip Buwa was instructed to work with him.

Buwa, one of the most cold-blooded shooters the underworld has witnessed, was the exact opposite of Dolas in many respects. Where Maya was aggressive and foul-mouthed, Buwa was calm and was seldom heard uttering an abusive word. Where Maya was all about talk and bluster, Buwa was about silent action. While Maya was power-hungry, Buwa was only concerned with shooting whoever it was he was told to shoot and take his share of the money.

'I don't think Buwa even liked Maya all that much. But the instructions to work with him had come directly from Rajan, and Buwa abided by them,' ACP Sunil Deshmukh, Dadar division, said. Deshmukh was part of the Anti Terrorist Squad formed by now retired inspector general of police, Aftab Ahmed Khan, who at the time was additional commissioner of police in the ATS. The ATS team later shot Dolas dead in the now famous Lokhandwala encounter.

Maya's style of talking, which was uncouth and intimidating at the same time, coupled with his fear factor, soon made him the man of choice to be assigned the job of extortion calls. Dawood started providing a list of targets to be extorted, and Maya would dial number after number every day. It is said that his targets would be visibly shaken by the time the conversations were over. Money started flowing in smoothly, and people started fearing Maya as much as they feared Dawood.

In the beginning, a few businessmen did not pay up, refusing to take this new, young upstart seriously. Maya dealt with them by barging into their offices and pumping bullet after bullet in the furniture around them, leaving them cowering in fear. A couple of such firing jobs cemented Maya's image as someone not to be trifled with.

Dolas took this to be a sign of his growing power, and Dawood and Rajan, while making the most of the fear that Dolas struck in their targets' hearts, let him believe his delusion. His recent crimes and aggressive behavior was the perfect combination to scare targets into paying whatever amount was demanded. Soon, he became the face of the gang's extortion racket in the city.

The Bissi Bravura

The 'bissi' rackets were also a rage in the city at the time. There is no English word for 'bissi'. The rackets involved a group of people pooling in equal amounts of money at the beginning of every month. Because, when it first started, twenty men contributed, it was named bissi—in Hindi, *bees* means twenty. At the end of the month, there would be a lucky draw and the person whose name came up would get the entire kitty. So the draw was called the raising of bissi. Once your name came up in the lucky draw, however, you were automatically disqualified from throwing your name in the next draw, so that every participating member had at least one chance of winning the kitty. However, you had to keep contributing to the pool every month so that the total amount was not affected.

Bissi rackets involved amounts ranging from a few hundreds rupees to a few lakh, depending on who the participants were. Each bissi was managed by an operator who kept track of payments, debts, etc.

The smaller bissis were held among residents of the same chawl, while the medium-sized ones were between groups of small and medium businessmen dealing in the same goods or operating in the same area. The really serious bissis were played by the bigger businessmen, particularly those who imported smuggled goods under the aegis of the D-gang, and contributions were rarely less than fifty thousand rupees. Dawood's name, by default, contributed a sense of power to the bissi operators. In those days, cricket-betting and horse-race rigging had not even been conceived of.

The very nature of the rackets depended on every participating member paying every month, because if even one member refused to pay, the entire system would collapse. For this, a strong persuading factor was required, and for the businessmen connected to Dawood, '*bhai ka naam*' was as good a persuader as any. Those dense enough to refuse to pay were paid a little visit by Maya Dolas. This gave Maya a chance to further establish himself as a name to be feared. He produced results and produced them fast. The sight of Maya Dolas barging in through the door spewing abuses and threats was enough for anyone to start sweating and do whatever the hell it was that Dawood wanted you to do.

This, however, did not apply to the medium-sized bissis which did involve some serious amounts of money, though not at quite as high a level as the bigger ones. When a participant in a medium-sized bissi failed to pay up in a particular month, the entire operation came crashing down, leading to the other contributors getting furious over being robbed of their chance to win the pool.

It was one of these disgruntled bissi contributors who paved the way for the D-gang to enter the bissi racket in a more active way. He approached a D-gang member from that he knew his area and told him about the losses he was facing because another contributor, a businessman from central Mumbai, had failed to pay that month's instalment. The enterprising member took it up with his higher-ups. Maya and his men were sent to visit the defaulting contributor one fine morning and they spent a couple of hours explaining to him the consequences of not paying up. Maya began with telling the businessman that 'bhai' wanted him to pay the instalment, and continued to outline in great detail, peppered with curse words, the damage he would inflict on each of the businessman's loved ones if he did not pay up that very minute. The businessman called every number in his phonebook till he had scraped together the amount, and Maya walked out with the full instalment in cash, as well as a promise to never default on a payment again.

Thanks to neighbours who had seen Maya barge into the businessman's house, as well as other contributors who were part of the bissi scheme, news about what he had done spread within a day to other bissis in the city. Within a month, if one of the members of your bissi club failed to pay for whatever reason, Maya Dolas was the man you consulted for redressal of the grievance.

A couple of months later, another bissi club member approached Maya, but for a different reason. The man had suffered losses in his business that month and was not in a position to pay the month's instalment. Facing pressure from his fellow members, the man decided to act before they took the D-way. He went to Maya, narrated his woes and begged for protection, offering to pay whatever he could afford as well as pledging lifelong allegiance to him. Maya was getting money as well as respect, two things he valued the most, and he liked the proposition.

When the bissi club met the next time, the man walked in with Maya and his men behind him. Maya told everyone present that under no circumstances was his friend to be pressurized for that month's instalment. Nobody argued.

In a matter of days, bissi club members were falling over each other to win Maya's favour. Maya revelled in the respect and showered his graces to the highest bidder. Dawood, on his part, let Maya help recover bissi money or settle pending payment disputes. He delivered speedy and effective results, and this only strengthened Dawood's grip on the city.

Manhunt for Maya

It was around this time that A. A. Khan's ATS started taking an interest in Maya, as violent criminals with multiple murders to their name were exactly who they had come together to eliminate. Over the next two months, Khan's team made inquiries with Maya's friends, family members and targets and tapped scores of ground-level informants. People who were reported to be connected to the D-gang or had been seen in Maya's company even once were picked up and grilled. The work was slow, as not many were willing to cooperate for fear of Maya finding out. But slowly and patiently, the ATS built up a picture of Maya's personality as well as his habits.

By this time, Maya, too, had started taking all the precautions that a wanted man needed to take. Taking a page out of Ashok Joshi's book, Maya and his gang never stayed in one place for more than two to three days. There was no dearth of places for them to hide, as builders close to the gang always had vacant flats in their buildings or spaces to stay in their under-construction projects. While some offered these spaces to Maya to curry favour with the gang, others did it out of sheer fear. It would have taken a really stupid builder to say no to Maya Dolas in 1991, and builders, as a rule, are a smart lot. Maya kept moving between Mumbai and

Thane, and would call his targets to his hiding places to extort money from them, settle disputes or get them to do his bidding.

The ATS began closing in on Maya's gang in November 1991, and, on several occasions, Maya would flee from his hideout in the nick of time, with hardly an hour between his hasty exit and the ATS' arrival. The time gap kept getting shorter. Maya, too, stepped up his security measures, and often changed his location several times in a day.

Once the ATS learned that he was hiding in Palghar and left for the spot. Maya and his men somehow found out and left from Palghar a short while after they had reached. They came back to Mumbai and the ATS followed his trail to Lokhandwala Complex in the suburb of Andheri in northwest Mumbai.

For the next two days, an ATS team kept round-the-clock surveillance on an under-construction building in the Swati Apartment building complex, owned by builder Gopal Rajwani, following a tip-off that Maya was holed up there. Even as the police were winding up their surveillance, putting it down to faulty intelligence, they got another tip-off saying that he was very much in Lokhandwala, but in a different building in the complex. Deshmukh, Zunjarrao Gharal and M. A. Qavi sped to the building and were soon joined by the entire ATS, including A. A. Khan, Iqbal Sheikh Pramod Rane and Raja Mandge.

Swati Apartment stood in the northwest corner of the Apna Ghar complex and had two wings. The ATS' information was that Maya was holed up in flat number five in the A wing of the building. The first confirmation of Maya's presence in the building was in the form of a white Maruti Esteem, a vehicle that Buwa was known to drive.

The ATS team stopped a short discreet distance away from the building and Qavi sketched out a rough map of the area after a short recce. The police had observed that the flat was the only one that had two exits: one which opened onto the compound and another near a staircase. While Qavi, Gharal and Deshmukh headed to the exit that opened onto the compound, Rane Mandge and Sheikh went to the other exit. The men only paused to distribute bullet-proof vests among themselves. On realizing that there were only five vests, Sheikh said he didn't want one. Gharal too said he wouldn't take one. The team suited up and headed to their respective positions.

Sheikh, who was leading his team, reached the door to the flat and waited for the signal from Qavi, who, it was decided, would make the first move. Even as Sheikh was listening to an exchange of dialogues between two characters of the Amitabh Bachchan starrer *Akela* that was drifting out through the door, he heard his signal in the form of sudden gunfire. The operation was on.

Qavi, who had stormed in through the other door with Gharal and Deshmukh on his heels, came face-to-face with Buwa, who was sprawled out on a chair, his revolver next to him. In his trademark style, Buwa, without uttering a word, without so much as snarling at the intruders, made his move. The revolver seemed to suddenly appear in his hand as if by magic and started spewing out bullets in flashes of fire. As the policemen were in plainclothes, Buwa wasn't even sure if they were cops or rival gangsters. All he cared about was that they had kicked down his door, had guns in their hands and those guns were pointed at him.

Gharal, who was not wearing a bulletproof vest, was hit in the chest, while Qavi took a bullet in the arm. Bleeding heavily, Qavi, with Deshmukh's help, dragged Gharal out of the flat while simultaneously pumping bullets at Buwa, who was still firing with no expression on his face.

The furious policemen regrouped outside the building and got on their wireless sets. Within minutes, the message was conveyed to the entire Mumbai police force. They had been attacked. Two of their own were seriously injured. Payback had to be swift and unforgiving. Even as Gharal was being rushed to the hospital, policemen from all over the city were going for their armories before rushing out to their vehicles so that they could all converge on the battlefield that was the Lokhandwala complex.

The P-gang versus the D-gang

The police force is the most political and conflict-ridden department in the country but whenever they are under attack by outsiders they stand united against the onslaught. There are many such instances—they showed exemplary team spirit during the 26/11 attacks, and they displayed the same solidarity in November '91. It was not just Khan's men standing against Maya Dolas and the gang now. It was now the entire police force; the P-gang against the D-gang.

Amidst all the chaos, Qavi managed to convey one thing clearly. He had seen Dolas inside the flat. A full three months after his audacious escape from the Mazgaon court, Maya was to come face-to-face with the police in the Swati building.

The police took their positions in the building compound, every gun pointed at flat number five of the A Wing. At the helm of the army stood Khan, shirt open down the front, pistol tucked into the front of his waistband, loudspeaker in hand. Khan later told a television channel that, while his open shirt front served to add to his Dirty Harry image and became part of the legend, the real reason behind it was that his shirt buttons would not close easily over his bulletproof vest, and fastening his buttons was the last thing on his mind at the time.

Through the loudspeaker, Khan called out to Maya and his men, and told them that they had one chance to surrender. Minutes later, Buwa and another man emerged from one of the two exits and ran for his Esteem. Ducking low, he opened fire at the policemen while trying to reach his car. Scores of guns boomed out in near-perfect unison in response as the policemen returned fire from so many sides that Buwa and his companion were dead before they hit the ground. They never made it beyond a few meters from the door.

Khan and his team then turned their attention to Maya. Local residents had informed the police that the two wings of the Swati building were connected by a terrace. A team was sent up to the terrace through the B Wing so that they could access the A wing. Apparently the gangsters had had the same idea. Even as the police team advanced down the floors in the A wing, Gopal Pujari and Raju Nadkarni, two of Maya's men, came running up the stairs hoping to use the terrace to get away. The police opened fire without hesitating. Nadkarni went down in a hail of lead on the second floor stairs. The furious policemen didn't even pause as they stepped over his body, followed Pujari to the first floor, and shot him down.

Outside, Khan continued his warnings to Maya, telling him that there was no escape and that surrender was his only option. As Nadkarni and Pujari went down, Maya and Anil Pawar emerged from the flat. In full view of the policemen, who were just waiting for the duo to start something, the two gangsters raised the AK-47 assault rifles in their hands. Before they could even align their weapons to fire them, hundreds of bullets went through their bodies. Their blood began flowing in all directions through the scores of holes in their bodies almost as soon as they crashed down to the ground. The police slowly advanced, Khan in the lead, and surrounded Maya. They all watched, guns ready, as the life ebbed out of him.

'Maya was injured, he was bleeding, he was weak.

But he still died the same way he lived, with a snarl on his face and a curse on his lips,' Deshmukh recounted.

The police then entered the building and stormed flat number five, looking for Anil Khubchandani, the only one unaccounted for. He was found dead in a pool of bullet casings and his own blood in the middle of the flat which, like most of the ground floor, was pockmarked with bullets. The unidentified man who was shot down along with Buwa was later identified as Vijay Chakor, a constable posted with the Yerawada Central Jail in Pune. While there have been theories and counter-theories over the years, what he was doing there remains anybody's guess.

More than 2,500 bullets were fired in the operation, which lasted for four-and-a-half hours. The official term for what happened at the Lokhandwala Complex on that November afternoon was 'encounter'—defined as an armed face-off between policemen and criminals. In reality, what had transpired, on live television no less, was war. A clear message had been given out by the police: no matter who you think you are; you shoot at us, we shoot you down.

For six hours, the BBC covered the entire operation live, something that would only repeat itself during the terror attacks in Mumbai in 2008 which, incidentally, also occured in November. The footage aired by the BBC showed the entire locality struggling to calm down long after the operation was over. Women were crying, children were screaming, men were trying to comfort their families while wiping the sweat off their faces.

The aftermath was almost anti-climactic. Deshmukh drove to the D.N. Nagar police station and, as per procedure, registered a formal complaint against Maya and the five other dead men. They were booked for attempt to murder, attempt to commit murder of police officers by dangerous weapons, deterring public servants from discharging their duties and unlawful assembly. The last section left even some policemen chuckling as the FIR was finetuned. The Indian Penal Code designates an assembly of five or more persons as 'unlawful', 'if the common object of the persons composing that assembly', the IPC quotes, is a show of criminal force, to resist the execution of any law or to commit any other offence. While what Maya and his men did that afternoon overshoots every word of this definition, it is, nevertheless, a section that is applicable by law. One can only imagine the moment of dark amusement that police might have gone through while adding the section to the FIR.

Gharal, who was rushed to the Hinduja Hospital, recovered from his injuries and retired as ACP, Vakola division, in 2015. The entire team was recommended for Gallantry Awards, but the commendation was soon overshadowed by controversy following allegations and questions about the authenticity of the encounter. A petition was subsequently filed in the Bombay High Court, which the HC dismissed.

Some say it was a tip-off from informants that brought the police to the building. Others allege that it was Dawood who gave the order to eliminate Dolas as he was getting too big for his boots, to the extent of disrespecting Dawood. But almost everyone agrees that Maya's growing arrogance and escalating criminal activity in the city was the cause of his downfall. It either angered the police, rubbed someone close to Dawood the wrong way or incurred the wrath of Dawood himself.

Another theory is that Dolas was a casualty of the rift between Dawood and Rajan, which had begun brewing in 1991. Rajan later gave an interview to a television news channel, in which he claimed that Dawood had started picking off the shooters recruited by and loyal to Rajan in order to cut him down to size.

Meanwhile, there was the mystery of the seventy lakh rupees which Dolas apparently had in his possession which had gone missing. No one could locate the money or even offer an opinion on where it had gone. All speculation seemed to indicate the involvement of the ATS officers who actually risked their lives to contain the shooters that day.

Whatever the case, the encounter gave a much-needed boost to then police commissioner S. Ramamurthy's career. The now-retired cop had been at the receiving end of daily brickbats over the ever-rising menace of the underworld and the increasingly-frequent murders—a by-product of gang wars—being committed in broad daylight. Maya Dolas contributed in no small part to this, and the Lokhandwala encounter cemented Ramamurthy's image as the man under whose leadership the police had given a fitting reply to the criminal underworld of the city.

In death, Dolas gave a new lease of life to Ramamurthy's career.

HITMAN 5

The Mama of Maharashtrian Mafia

The Graph of Girangaon

A monolithic business entity with several big companies working under the aegis of the same leader is often referred as a megacorporation. And mafia gangs in Mumbai are like megacorps. There were many ganglords, smugglers and underworld chieftains before Dawood Ibrahim set foot in the Mumbai mafia. But it is he who has the dubious distinction of corporatizating the underworld.

Dawood compartmentalized gang operations and made his henchmen managers of each wing of his several businesses. Dawood totally decentralized the command structure and stepped in only when his intervention was absolutely necessary. Thus, there was someone to look after the extortion business; another to oversee film territories abroad; a group focused on money-laundering and money-cleansing in India; one section in charge of cricket-betting, horse-racing and fixing sports....

However, most other gangs believed in a centralized

command, with the leaders ruling over their men with an iron fist. Their insecurity that their henchmen would topple them and take over the gang would not allow them to delegate powers to their managers.

Among all the gang leaders, Arun Gawli was the most insecure one. He never wanted to share his power and authority. Even when he was imprisoned, he handed over the reins of his gang to his wife Asha Gawli. Unfortunately, while Asha Gawli was a highly venerable figure in the hierarchy, managing a gang with its multifarious operations was beyond her capacity.

Gawli's frequent incarceration and his constant hide-and-seek with the law all fuelled the aspirations of the second-rung members in his gang. While Gawli was focused on carving a niche for himself in politics, his lieutenants began earning their stripes and registered their upward climb in the gang.

'They are called "*sikkas*" in the underworld lexicon. A currency that keeps the gang's name going in the market. For every gang, there is at least one sikka at any given time that the gang capitalizes on. For more than seven years, Arun Gawli's sikka was Sadanand Pawle,' a Crime Branch officer said. Gawli trusted Pawle because he did not embezzle money, and kept up the gang's fear quotient in people's minds,

Pawle, like several mobsters, joined the gang due to unemployment and the frustration of a jobless youth unable to feed his family.

The infamous mill strike of 1982 had rewritten the destiny of the city with blood, gore, violence, death and a relentless cycle of crime.

Dr. Datta Samant, a reluctant union leader, had announced a textile mill strike in 1982, resulting in the displacement of over 250,000 workers who had a long history of strikes under the presumption that there would eventually be a rationalization of wages on par with that of other industries. At the time of the strike, a skilled textile worker was drawing Rs. 1,500 while an unskilled worker was drawing Rs. 700/800.

The mills had begun a downward spiral long before Dr. Samant called the strike. The textile workers, who knew they were underpaid as compared to workers in the pharmaceutical or engineering industries, decided to approach him to take up their case. They were tired of the official industry union, the Rashtriya Mill Mazdoor Sangh (RMMS), which was affiliated to the Congress-I, and had failed to take up their cause. Dr. Samant had fought for workers in other industries, and had a great fan following because his agitations always resulted in unheard of wage hikes. He was reluctant to call for a textile workers' strike as it was not his field of work. But the workers surrounded his house in Ghatkopar and refused to leave until he buckled.

The fact that many companies, which initially had pleaded an inability to increase wages later agreed to pay more, added to Samant's and the workers' resolve not to let the balance sheets come in the way of their 'exorbitant' demands.

The strike received national coverage. The government of the day refused to budge despite the economic losses suffered by the city and the industry. The eighteen-month mill strike, one of the longest in India's labour history, proved to be the death knell of the already-struggling textile mills. Most of them shut down or moved their plants outside the city after the strike collapsed. Three lakh textile mill workers lost their jobs.

By this time, there were hardly any textile mills running to full capacity, and international brands like Finlay's, Calico and Binny's lapsed into history. Though the strike was blamed, every mill had its own reason for closure. Some closed because of the competition that was the result of globalization, some because they were labour-intensive and others because of family feuds.

The workers in the mills were predominantly Maharashtrians from south Raigad and Ratnagiri. The Konkan coast was very poor in those days, and farmers had to fall back on one rice crop and mangoes. Thus, the cotton mills were the warp and weft of the migrant's life. For trade unionism, they would align with the communists, but as the communists did not believe in religion or culture, the workers soon came under the sway of the right-wing Shiv Sena. The Shiv Sena found its early cadres amongst the mill workers of the Konkan region.

There were also workers from other Indian states who eventually put down roots here. Slowly, chawls that were just ten minutes' walking distance from the mills evolved into multicultural spaces driven by common middle-class values.

The chawls and two-storeyed tenements, like the BDD chawls at Worli, housed workers in small and cramped rooms. Alcoholism was rampant, as was money-lending. Bootleggers and *matka* dens thrived. To escape the squalid living conditions, workers and their children spent much of their time outside the house. Children lived and survived on their wits. Sociologists talk of communalism breeding here.

But there was something else that was being bred—organized crime. Gawli worked in Shakti Mills (the now infamous mills where a young photojournalist was gang-raped on 28 August 2013), following in the tradition of his parents. The family of another Maharashtrian ganglord, Amar Naik, sold vegetables in Dadar, but his parents worked in the mills. Gangster D. K. Rao's parents worked in a mill, as did the parents of Anil Parab. By the early '90s, the Maharashtrian and non-Maharashtrian boys who grew up in Girangaon (the village of mills), working their way up the mafia ladder by stabbing and killing for money, realized that they were sitting on a goldmine.

South Mumbai was cramped and bursting at its seams and there was no place for expansion. The Bandra-Kurla Complex was being promoted as an alternative, but it lacked proximity to south Mumbai.

The real-estate mavens, the mafia and the politicians realized that the only way for Mumbai to go was south-central. Girangaon had to make way for the new face of Mumbai, probably the next financial nerve centre of the city. One by one, the mills that had survived Dr. Samant's strike closed. The money at stake was running into crores. Some mills were sold for four hundred crore rupees onwards and others were pegged at six hundred to nine hundred crore.

By the '90s, Girangaon had become the next Kurukshetra.

The big players like Dawood had aligned with the builders, while the Gawlis aligned with the mill owners. Everybody benefited, except the mill workers. And the new players, both among the mafia and Maharashtra's politics—and possibly even the politics of New Delhi—would come from the money of Girangaon.

Pawle's Promotion

Sada Pawle, like his peers, was the product of despair and penury.

A little over five-and-a-half feet, but very muscular in build, with a perpetually menacing look on his face, Pawle channelized his pent-up physical energies and sense of a hopeless future into crime. Pawle and his imposing physique became the epitome of power. All Pawle had to do was to make a phone call and the person at the other end would start quaking in his shoes.

The youngest of three siblings, Pawle had an elder sister, Hausabai, and a brother Anand, who worked in Central Railways. Anand eventually got married and moved out of the family home to live in Central Railway quarters, while Hausabai, too, got married and went to live with her husband, Gundu Tawde.

Dagdi Chawl old-timers remember Pawle as a young mill worker who stayed near Gawli and played kabaddi very well. Kabaddi was among the more popular sports played by residents of the chawl and Pawle, when he was not busy beefing up his physique in the chawl's gymnasium, would play on Rama Naik's team. Whenever the team had a disagreement with whoever was playing against them, Pawle was the first to get aggressive.

Pawle's belligerent tendencies soon became his signature in Dagdi Chawl, and word spread around that he was not someone you wanted to get into a fight with.

Like hundreds of mill workers in the 1980s, Pawle was drawn into a life of crime partly due to sheer frustration over the ongoing disputes between the unions and the mill owners, but also because of the lure of money. People like Naik and Gawli were getting famous, throwing around money and living in style, and everyone wanted to be like them.

Pawle was recruited into the gang by Gawli's mentor, Rama Naik, in 1987, along with others like Dilip Kulkarni and Bandya Adivarekar. The gang survived mainly on extortions, and there was a constant need for henchmen like these to pay a visit to businessmen who thought defying the gang was a good idea.

In a year, Pawle was among the favourite musclemen of the gang. He was short-tempered, scary and his blows hurt. What more could a boss ask for in a henchman?

In July 1987, Naik was killed in an encounter by sub-inspector Rajendra Katdhare. Naik was at a saloon in Chembur getting a haircut when Katdhare reached the spot. There are some who suspect that Dawood Ibrahim, who had already moved to Dubai and had started eliminating his rivals one by one, played a role in Katdhare learning about Naik's whereabouts the day he was killed.

The Byculla area was at the time ruled by a triumvirate of gangsters: Naik, Gawli and Babu Reshim. That same year, Reshim was killed by Vijay Utekar, a D-gang member who had been severely beaten up by Reshim a couple of years earlier over a local dispute. Dawood sought out the revenge-hungry Utekar, befriended him, and put a gun in his hands. Utekar took care of the rest. In one of the most daring murders in the history of the city, he stormed into a police cell at the Jacob Circle jail and shot Reshim dead inside the lock-up. The stunningly audacious murder included lobbing grenades at the police lock-up to blow open its doors.

With this, the reins of the gang fell to Gawli, who became the undisputed king of Byculla and nearby areas. A lot of the henchmen who earlier worked under Reshim and Naik began working for him. Among these was Sada Pawle, whose propelment to a place of such importance in the gang would have perhaps surprised himself as well.

Pawle was as merciless as he was cold-blooded. The true mark of an inhumane killer, according to several Crime Branch officers, is the way he kills. It is easier to point a gun at someone and pull the trigger, they say, than to stab someone repeatedly while geysers of blood erupt from his body till life has drained out. It takes real nerve to be able to keep stabbing your target while he is writhing and screaming in pain, and even more so to keep doing it till the final scream; much harder than squeezing off a few rounds from a gun at a distance and running away before the target has even hit the ground.

Of the eight to ten cases of murder and extortion that were registered against Pawle in his lifetime, the first few were committed with daggers. Pawle only started using guns later on in his career, when the underworld started procuring sophisticated pistols and AK assault rifles. His preference for using blades and his bare hands was one of the reasons why he became a name that struck fear in the hearts of people. They never knew when Pawle was going to get angry and pounce upon them.

Pawle's Powerplay

An apocryphal story is related about a top politician in Thane who made several statements against Gawli. The story goes that Pawle managed to enter his office in a casual manner, uncocked his gun, kept it on the table and began staring at the politician without blinking. The politician, who had heard about Pawle's reputation and was well-known for his bravado and arrogant swagger in the corridors of power, could not stand Pawle's icy stare beyond a minute. He didn't say a word lest Pawle pick up the gun and empty the whole magazine into him. Subsequent to the meeting, the politician never dared to utter a word against Gawli.

By 1990, Pawle had become Arun Gawli's sikka. Gawli knew that if he sent Pawle on a job, he did not need to worry about it getting done. First, a henchman would call the target and tell him that he was speaking on behalf of Sada Pawle. If that was not enough for the target to start sweating in rivulets, Pawle himself would speak to him. If the target showed even a hint of defiance, Pawle would pay him a visit. Defiance was something that Pawle had no patience with.

Pawle also proved his loyalty to Gawli in 1990 when the latter was seething with the intense desire to avenge his brother Pappa's murder in Mahim. Using all his contacts and goodwill, Gawli found out the name of the man in whose name the car used in the killing was registered.

Gawli then told Pawle that he wanted this man—Manoj Kulkarni—at any cost. Pawle spread out a dragnet to catch Kulkarni and the efforts paid off when Pawle learned that Kulkarni was coming to Mumbai to attend a wedding in his family.

Pawle found out where Kulkarni was staying and, on the morning of the wedding, as Kulkarni was about to leave, Pawle, along with his trusted aide Vijay Tandel and two others, reached the spot in a white Ambassador car, wearing formal shirts and trousers. The Ambassador was an official police vehicle back then, and the formal shirt and trousers are still associated with policemen in plain clothes.

Posing as Crime Branch officers, Pawle and his team told Kulkarni that he needed to be questioned and bundled him into the car. Kulkarni was indeed questioned, but not in any police establishment.

Pawle took him straight to Dagdi Chawl and subjected him to a brutal interrogation. His screams echoed throughout the room specially designated for '*chaukashi*', the Marathi word for inquiry, till Kulkarni, between sobs, admitted to having participated in Pappa's murder. He was then bundled into the same Ambassador car that had brought him there, taken to Tardeo, shot dead, and his body left on the road for the world to see.

Around this time, Pawle began to be called Sada Mama by the gang. While the nickname might not sound all that impressive, it conveyed the amount of respect that he commanded. Gawli was called Daddy and his brother Pappa. Arun Gawli's wife Asha automatically became Mummy. Aside from Gawli and his family, Pawle was the only one the gang deemed worthy enough for a respectful nickname.

For Sada Mama, the next turning point came in 1990 when the police raided Daddy's house following a tip-off that he was behind Kulkarni's murder. After an exhaustive search, an AK-47 assault rifle was found hidden inside a sofa in one of the rooms.

The single weapon was enough for the police to arrest Gawli and charge him under the Terrorist and Disruptive Activities (TADA) Act, a serious charge. At the time, the police had started cracking down on the underworld's weaponry after learning that the gangs had recently procured a consignment of AK-47s and AK-56s from Afghanistan.

Gawli was tried and convicted under the TADA, and was sentenced to imprisonment for seven years. 'Gawli's jail term elevated Pawle to a position of power. He practically ran the gang while Gawli was in jail, and he did so with an iron hand,' says retired assistant commissioner of police Jaywant Hargude.

A couple of months after Gawli was sent to jail, Pawle called up a builder, named a sum and asked him to keep it ready. The builder was one of several who were extorted by Gawli on a regular basis. As with a lot of such people, the builder thought he was a 'friend' of Daddy's. When Pawle called the second time, the builder told him that his arrangement was with Gawli, and he would only pay the top boss. Pawle hung up without saying a word.

The same day, Pawle's men barged into the builder's office, dragged him to their car, and took him to Dagdi Chawl. The builder was taken screaming and kicking into a room in one corner of the chawl where Pawle personally thrashed him to within an inch of his life with his bare hands. The builder's loud pleas for mercy were audible far outside the room, telling everyone two things: never take Mama lightly, and never be arrogant with him.

Finally the cries stopped, the door to the room opened, and Pawle walked out of the room, gently massaging his knuckles. He walked straight to his house, even as people fell over themselves to get out of his way, and went to the phone. Settling down on his chair as if nothing had happened, Pawle dialled the builder's residence and told his son to come to Dagdi Chawl right away. The alarmed son sped to the chawl and Pawle calmly led him to the room where his father was lying in a pool of blood, alive, but lucky to be so.

Pawle then told the speechless son the amount that he

had demanded from his father and told him to get the amount immediately, after which he could take his father away. The son moved heaven and earth but arranged for every last penny so that he could take his father to a hospital before he succumbed to his injuries. Before he left, Pawle only told the son one more thing: do not tell the police. The son complied.

'Over the years, we received countless reports of Pawle assaulting and extorting businessmen in south Mumbai using brutal and ruthless methods. Had all of them approached us, the number of complaints against Pawle would have been close to a hundred,' Inspector Mahesh Desai remarks.

Word spread far and wide about what could happen if you made the mistake of saying no to Sada Mama. The extortion money started flowing in easily after that. The only ones who still dared to defy Pawle were the ones with ties to rival gangs or good connections with the Mumbai police. But even these connections did not faze Pawle, who continued to enforce his reign of terror.

In 1997, Gawli, who had by this time started making extortion calls while in jail, called builder Natwarlal Desai, alias Nathubhai, and asked him to pay extortion money to Pawle. Desai at first did not take the demand seriously and later flat out refused to pay. By this time, the gang war between Gawli and Dawood was on in full swing, and maintaining their fear factor in the minds of the people was as important for them as decimating each other's gang members. Tolerating a refusal from an extortion target was not an option for Gawli, and for

Pawle, whom Gawli called and spoke to about Desai's refusal, it was the ultimate insult.

Accompanied by three henchmen, Pawle drove to Desai's office in Nariman Point, pumped his body full of bullets, and walked out. While the murder in the plush south Mumbai location shook the city, for Pawle, it was just another day at work.

The Final Straw

But perhaps the most famous example of Pawle's ferocity was the murder of industrialist Vallabh Thakkar. One of the leading industrialists in the city at the time, Thakkar owned Raghuvanshi Mills and, according to reports, had used the Gawli gang's service to evict tenants from the houses he wanted to demolish in order to make way for his projects, in exchange for regular payments.

In 1997, Thakkar made two mistakes which would cost him his life. When Pawle contacted him and demanded fifty lakh rupees, a huge amount in those days, he refused to pay, asking him to accept less instead. Even worse, when Pawle persisted with his threats and demands, Thakkar complained to the police. The ultimate gesture of defiance angered Pawle so much that he became blind to everything except teaching Thakkar a lesson.

A terrified Thakkar appealed to the police to save him from an infuriated Pawle. Gawli was in jail at the time, and some senior police officers approached him to broker a deal on Thakkar's behalf.

The extortion rackets always ran on an understanding between the underworld, the police and the business fraternity. If the underworld chose a target who had connections in the right places, the police would step in and a compromise would be brokered. Everyone, including the underworld top bosses knew and followed this. The same understanding might have worked out for Thakkar, too, had he not registered a complaint against Pawle, something that inflicted a deep wound on the gangster's ego.

Gawli sent word to Pawle from the Arthur Road central jail, telling him that Thakkar was prepared to pay twenty-five lakh rupees, and that he should accept the money and let the matter end. Pawle sent word back saying that he would only accept fifty lakh rupees, and not a penny less. Further, he told Gawli, he would make sure that Thakkar paid the money or paid with his life.

'*Jau de na, Mama. Kashala adun basto?* (Let it be, Mama. Why are you being adamant?)' Gawli asked him.

'*Saalyani complaint ka keli? Aata nahi sodnar.* (Why did the bugger complain? Now I'm not letting him go),' Pawle responded.

And so it was that Pawle and two of his men barged into Thakkar's office and shot him dead in broad daylight.

What is significant about the incident, and this is something everyone from the Gawli gang to the Mumbai police took note of, is that Pawle openly defied Gawli's instructions. And even more importantly, Gawli let him get away with it. Even Gawli knew not to stand in the way of an enraged Pawle. Some even go as far as to say that Gawli—having seen Pawle's journey from an aggressive, short-tempered mill worker who got into fights over kabaddi matches, to a ruthless and feared chief lieutenant in the gang—was scared of Pawle.

His rising notoriety and the fast-spreading tales of what happens to people who cross Sada Mama earned him the ire of the Mumbai police, who pulled out all stops to stop him.

The late '90s was an era of instant justice for the police. They had seen enough instances where top lawyers hired by gangsters decimated public prosecutors in unequal battles and secured bail for their clients. Gawli himself had managed to make a mockery of the legal system of the country.

Pawle was Gawli's most powerful weapon, and equally elusive. The entire police force was after him. They did not mean to book Pawle, they wanted him dead. Despite the courts coming down heavily against extrajudicial killings, the police had decided to make him an example.

Top-notch encounter specialists like Pradeep Sharma, Praful Bhosale and Vijay Salaskar were given total freedom to track down Pawle and kill him. Never mind if it was in a crowded place and the killing was witnessed by hundreds of witnesses.

This kind of total support and freedom emboldened the trigger-happy executioners.

Crime Branch officers under Param Bir Singh, who was then deputy commissioner of police (crime), launched a manhunt for Pawle, who had, by this time, sensed the impending danger and started changing his location frequently and trusted no one.

In August 1997, the late Vijay Salaskar, who was then an assistant police inspector, received a tip-off that Pawle had come to Dagdi Chawl after weeks of being underground. Salaskar called in back-up and raided the chawl, but could not find Pawle despite an exhaustive search. Pawle, either because he learned about the raid or because of his cautious nature, had slipped out a short while before the police arrived.

Even as Salaskar was briefing his superiors about the failed raid, he received another tip-off: Pawle was at that moment heading out of the city along with his friend Vijay Tandel. Salaskar hurriedly put together a team consisting of himself and sub-inspectors Hemant Desai and Avinash Sawant, as well as several other officers and constables. The tip-off said that Pawle would be going to Rajawadi Hospital junction at Ghatkopar east before proceeding out of the city.

Salaskar, working further on the tip-off, found out that Pawle, his sister Hausabai, brother Anand and Anand's wife Anita, were going to Shirdi. Anand had asked one of his colleagues from the Central Railway, Baldevsingh Panesar, to accompany them. Panesar was joining them at Vidyavihar, as he stayed in the Central Railway headquarters there.

The informant had told Salaskar that the group would meet at Rajawadi junction and exit to Eastern Express to head to Shirdi. Acting swiftly and determined not to miss this time, Salaskar also stationed a back-up team at Mulund check *naka*.

Pawle's Fiat was intercepted near the Rajawadi Hospital by Salaskar's Maruti 100, while Sub-Inspector Subhash Mayekar stopped his own car behind the Fiat. The cops jumped out of their vehicles, guns trained. After this point, the sequence of events depends on who is doing the telling.

The police's version is that Pawle stepped out of the Fiat, anger written all over his scowling features, an AK-56 in his hand, and let loose with the deadly assault rifle, while Tandel, stepping out of his side of the car, opened fire with a pistol. Two constables were injured in the firing, and the entire police team returned fire, riddling both Pawle and Tandel with bullets.

According to the writ filed by Hausabai and Anand in court, though, the entire encounter was staged and Pawle and Tandel never stood a chance, as the plan was always to kill Pawle and not to arrest him, and Tandel just happened to be collateral damage.

The brother-sister duo submitted in court that the policemen descended on their Fiat and dragged Pawle and Tandel out, while the remaining occupants tried to save them. Hausabai, in her deposition, told the court that she was clinging to Pawle to save him, but he told her to let him go and save herself, after which Pawle and Tandel were shot dead in cold blood.

The matter went all the way to the Supreme Court, and in September 2014, the court delivered a verdict in favour of the police, ruling that the encounter was genuine.

HITMAN 6

The Ghost Who Killed

An Inclement Proposal

'*Apni behen ki pati ko jaan se maar do, phir main maan samjhunga tum mein koi baat hai* (Kill your sister's huband, and then I will know that there is something in you),' Chhota Shakeel's deep voice grunted on the other side of the line.

Sadiq Jalawar felt the ground slip from under his feet. He was aghast at what he had just heard. His face turned pale and his hands started trembling. He loved his sister. She had been happily married to her husband, Zulfikar, for years now, and Sadiq couldn't swallow the fact that he would have to widow his sister with his own hands.

It was such a high price to pay to join the army of killers that was the Chhota Shakeel gang. Tears began welling in his eyes. Sadiq's silence echoed on the phone. Shakeel told him to man up and do what was asked of him. He told Sadiq to call him only when Zulfikar was dead. Sadiq swallowed a glass of water that was on the table and told Shakeel the job would be done.

Sadiq decided that he would pull the trigger at point-blank range and scoot from the spot even before his beloved brother-in-law could collapse to the ground. Sadiq felt that if he could avoid seeing his brother-in-law in a pool of his own blood, life ebbing out of him slowly, eyes quieting, and death coming to him in gasps, perhaps then he could forgive himself.

But Shakeel wanted to test him thoroughly and was not willing to make any concessions. 'I don't want you to use a gun. I want you to kill him with a chopper,' he said.

Sadiq froze. How could he inflict stab wounds on his brother-in-law? And chopper injuries were excruciatingly painful. Victims shrieked with agony. The victim might not die with one stab of the chopper. It might require multiple attacks. The screams of pain, the victim's struggle to remain alive against a forced death was an unbearable sight for a relative to witness. Especially if they loved each other and there was an intense level of trust between the two of them. But Sadiq could not protest. He suppressed the rising bile in his mouth. And struggled to mouth two words.

'*Ji, Bhai.*'

Sadiq then hung up the phone and paced around the dark room. His mind faltered at the offer he had just accepted. Chhota Shakeel and his gang members had never taken Sadiq seriously. To prove them wrong, Jalawar had confronted Shakeel and asked for a chance to prove his worth. In return, Shakeel had proposed this idea. Sadiq knew Shakeel's intentions behind the task. Shakeel was aware of how much Sadiq loved his sister; he knew Sadiq would never do anything to hurt her. But times had changed and so had Sadiq. He was more ambitious than ever. He had just left Arun Gawli's gang and was determined to make a mark with Chhota Shakeel's company. Even if it came at the cost of widowing his own sister.

The same night, Sadiq called his sister. She was overjoyed to hear from her brother—it had been weeks since he had called. They had been very close growing up, and she returned the deep affection he had for her. Sadiq's voice choked with emotion, but he held on to his vision. His sister invited him over for dinner, which Sadiq politely turned down. He asked his sister for her husband. A confused Zulfikar came on the line. Sadiq told him he had some work with him and to meet him outside, by his gate. Zulfikar agreed and they hung up.

Zulfikar knew how close Sadiq was to his sister and he was surprised that he had refused to come home. Sadiq had never lied or disobeyed his sister before. Something was wrong, and Zulfikar was curious to find out what it could be.

Zulfikar immediately left his house and waited outside the gate. After a few minutes he saw the headlights of a bike coming his way. It was Sadiq. Zulfikar heaved a sigh of relief and greeted his brother-in-law. Sadiq hugged Zulfikar with one arm, and held the other—the one holding the chopper—behind his back. Zulfikar asked Sadiq what was wrong and why he wouldn't come inside the house. Sadiq was quiet. He stared at Zulfikar, his heart racing at what he was about to do.

'*Mujhe maaf kar dena, Bhaijaan* (Forgive me, brother),' Sadiq finally muttered. With that, he took out his chopper and struck Zulfikar with heavy blows. Sadiq stabbed him five times and pinned him to the ground. He waited over the writhing body of Zulfikar to see him breathe his last. When the bloodshot eyes of Zulfikar no longer held signs of life, Sadiq collapsed to his knees. He wailed loudly, his hands covering his face in shame at what he had done. He wept uncontrollably for minutes, and then wiped his tears and stood up. Sadiq took one last look at his sister's house, mounted his bike, and left.

Sadiq then called up Shakeel and informed him that the task was complete. He had single-handedly destroyed his sister's life and made her a widow. But that was a price he was willing to pay to earn Shakeel's respect.

Shakeel was shocked when Sadiq called with the news. Shakeel had expected him to call back with the report that he had changed his mind or a request for a different assignment. So when Sadiq called to say that he had killed his brother-in-law, stabbing him five times all over his body, Shakeel could not believe it. But he knew that Sadiq would not make a false claim. That day marked a transition for Sadiq. From Sadiq Jalawar, he now became Sadiq Kalia. Shakeel was so impressed with Sadiq that he invited him to Dubai to meet him.

Once there, Sadiq became an instant hit with the gang. Shakeel introduced Kalia to another gang member, Salim Chikna, and asked the two to team up. They later went on to form the infamous Kalia–Chikna duo. Chikna was an expert biker and could manoeuvre the machine however he wanted even in the midst of the most acute traffic congestion. He drove at a lightning speed and no police van had ever been able to catch up with him. It was a time of relentless and incessant killings by the duo. Both unleashed terror on Chhota Rajan's men in the mid-'90s. The duo has been credited with nearly twenty to twenty-five killings on the behest of Shakeel.

The ABS Demolisher

At the time, the political scenario in Mumbai was like a rollercoaster ride for politicians. Arun Gawli was no exception. Initially, it seemed as though things had brightened up for him. The Shiv Sena presented him as a Hindu don, pitting him against Dawood. Sena supremo Bal Thackeray had no qualms in siding with a don that was Maharashtrian—something he publically announced after his Dussehra rally in the aftermath of the 1993 riots. Gawli's association with the Shiv Sena gave him political patronage. But soon, Gawli began suspecting that Bal Thackeray was ignoring him and that the Sena were only using him for his Hindu name. Cracks in their relationship showed when Gawli ordered the killing of Thackeray's *manasputra* or godson, Jayant Jadhav, and Sena MLA Rameh More. Gawli believed that Jayant Jadhav was instrumental in Thackeray getting close to his rivals, the Ashwin Naik gang.

Jitendra Dabholkar, the head of the Kamgar Sena, went to met Arun Gawli in jail and convinced him to float a political party. And so Gawli went ahead and formed the Akhil Bharatiya Sena, which had its office inside the fortress-like walls of Dagdi Chawl. It challenged the original sons of the soil, Shiv Sena, on their home ground. Soon, he began to attract all the disgruntled workers from the Shiv Sena. When Gawli got back from jail, he became the president of ABS and Dabholkar became its secretary. The ABS not only stole into the Shiv Sena's votebank but also took over the Oberoi Hotels and Tata Memorial Hospital unions earlier affiliated with that party.

Within a year of its existence, the ABS had registered nearly 350,000 members in Maharashtra, with another 50,000 in the union. Gawli suddenly appeared as a messiah to the people. Increasingly, hordes of people made a beeline to his chawl to complain about their problems.

The growing political power of Gawli was unsettling for a lot of people. Particularly the D-Company. Gawli seemed to be getting stronger and stronger with both political and public support. Shakeel knew the man behind Gawli's strength was none other than Dabholkar. He was the backbone of ABS and eliminating him would leave Gawli handicapped. The only way to destroy Gawli's political clout was to undermine the growth of ABS. Shakeel picked up his phone and called for his finest shooters. Dabholkar had to be killed, he told them.

Shakeel pressed into service his sharpshooter army including Kalia, Munna Jhingada and Chikna. The trio received the orders and set to work. Munna followed Dabholkar for a few days and figured out his schedule.

Then, the three killers fixed a date to shoot Dabholkar dead. On the day, an unsuspecting Dabholkar left Dagdi Chawl as usual in his Armada car. He was aware he was under the scrutiny of the underworld, but never in his wildest dreams had he anticipated the fate that awaited him.

On the day, Chikna wasn't able to accompany Kalia. Munna asked Kalia to drop the plan—they needed a rider and it would be impossible to carry the killing without Chikna. But Kalia was determined to finish Dabholkar on the same day.

Kalia got on to his bike and started following the Armada car. He got close to Dabholkar on the Milan subway. With a stretch of slums on either side, and with new buildings towering over the road, the Milan subway is one of the busiest turns in the city. Swarming with people at all times, vehicles struggle to make their way through it. It was unimaginable for any shooter to carry out a killing in this complex mess. But Kalia was not just any shooter. He was determined to finish Dabholkar at all costs. He followed Dabholkar's car at a close distance. After crossing the subway, the Armada car took a turn towards Santacruz. At that point, Dabholkar asked his driver to stop the car because he had to meet somebody. Dabholkar then stepped out of his car, closely shadowed by his bodyguard.

From a distance of a few metres, Kalia spotted Dabholkar getting out of his car. He was standing with his bodyguard on the sidewalk, looking around for someone. Kalia rode up. This was his chance to shoot

Dabholkar down and finish what he had come for. Kalia parked his bike and headed towards Dabholkar with his gun in hand. He approached a puzzled Dabholkar, who quickly turned pale at the sight of the gun. In a split second, Kalia opened fire and shot Dabholkar and his bodyguard dead. Kalia then rushed back to his bike, and sped off into the crowd.

Kalia thus managed to not only shoot down one of the city's most promising politicians in broad daylight, but also executed the killing in one of the busiest streets in Mumbai. This was perhaps the most sensational killing done by any shooter at that time. After Dabholkar's murder, Sadiq Kalia was the most-wanted criminal in the city and the Mumbai police started a hunt for him.

Dabholkar's killing finished the budding political career and ambitions of Arun Gawli. He was devastated. Whe he learnt that the killing was the handiwork of a young man who started off from his own team, he cursed his lack of strategic foresight.

Kalia's Gangland Training

Born in Agripada, Sadiq spent most of his childhood with his friends in Dagdi Chawl playing football. He had seen the famed gangster around from when he was a child, and would always imitate him. He loved how Gawli controlled his men and idolized the gangster's ways. In the coming years, Sadiq expressed his desire to join the Gawli gang. Through friends he got a meeting arranged with 'Daddy', who promised him some work. Sadiq was made to join a group that collected extortion money for Gawli. He also sold cinema tickets in black at Palace Cinema in Byculla. Sadiq did not like his initial work but presumed that was how one graduated from being a low-level to top-level gangster. Sadiq hung on to the work despite his reservations.

Around the same time, Gawli had recruited other unemployed young boys to carry out his *hafta* operations. They were all put in groups to visit hotels, shops and offices around Byculla to gather intelligence and shortlist prospective extortion victims. Owners who refused to pay were beaten up. This caused fear in the area and others started paying up without protest. Sadiq found this petty job demeaning to his ambitions. He did not like his status as a *hafta wasuli* person or a black-ticket seller. He believed in his potential and wanted to be part of Gawli's core teamof. He craved the power and status that came with being a prominent member of the gang. Sadiq was not only ambitious but also knew the art of perseverance; however, after a period of unsuccessfully trying to get the attention of Arun Gawli, Sadiq finally quit the gang. Little did he know that better doors would soon open for him—a few months later, Sadiq joined the D-Company.

Shakeel believed in the young lanky man and entrusted him with some of the most important assignments of the D-Company. He was no longer the '*bachcha*' that Shakeel once thought him to be. Sadiq was now one of the most feared men in the underworld mafia. In police circles he was nicknamed 'Bhoot' because he was as stealthy as a ghost on the move. He would appear on a scene, finish his business, and leave without a trace. Moreover, his extremely dark skin helped him camouflage himself in the dark.

He was also nicknamed 'Narsimha', after the half-lion avatar of Lord Vishnu. He was strong and fearless like the avatar, and ruthless with his weapons. In the underworld, a shooter or an operative is usually given only one sobriquet. Sadiq became one of the only hitmen to have several, including Kalia, Bhoot and Narsimha.

Sadiq, Salim Chikna and Munna Jhingada operated like a mini-army. They divided up the tasks: Munna would do the groundwork and follow the trails of the targets. Based on this information, Chikna and Kalia would carry out the murders. They successfully gunned down many men from rival gangs.

However, there was one assignment in particular that Kalia could never complete. It was killing none other than his own former boss, Arun Gawli.

When he was given the assignment to murder Gawli, Kalia couldn't contain his excitement. He made elaborate plans to finally avenge the humiliating treatment that Gawli had meted out to him during his early mafia days. Sadiq had information that Gawli, who then resided in Pune, would be travelling to Mumbai to address a gathering. Kalia planned to attend the gathering and shoot Gawli dead in front of all his supporters. He made a detailed plan with his partner Chikna for this, but as fate would have it, Gawli was tipped off about Shakeel's plan and he cancelled the meeting. Kalia's dream of killing Gawli himself never materialized. Kalia waited for hours, but Gawli never showed up.

The Khaki versus Kalia

Sadiq Kalia had induced fear in the city with his macabre and daring killings and the police had been after him for some time. One particular murder turned the police heat on him.

Kushal Jain was a moneylender who operated from Mahim. Kushal and Kalia had been good friends in the past, but Kushal did not approve of his friend's links with the underworld. Kushal shared a deep personal rapport with Inspector Pradeep Sharma and went on to join hands with the police as an informant. He would also pass on crucial information about Kalia to the police. Kalia felt betrayed by his friend and decided to avenge his disloyalty.

It was the last day of the Ganapati visarjan. The entire city was high on festive spirits after the ten-day long celebrations. Kushal Jain was in his office at Mahim. He had decided to leave for home early, before the city roads were packed with visarjan traffic. Around mid-afternoon Kushal got up, ready to leave. It was then that Sadiq swiftly walked into his office. Kushal trembled at the sight. He knew Kalia had not come bearing good news and that his life was in danger. Kalia calmly sat down on a chair opposite Kushal. A shaking Kushal begged

Kalia to spare his life and let him go. Kalia let Kushal whimper and beg for his life. Suddenly, in a swift, cold-blooded move, Kalia sprayed an array of bullets right into his former friend's body. The lifeless body of Kushal slumped back into the chair. Kalia got up, took one last look at the bloodied body of his friend, and walked away.

Kushal Jain's killing was a challenge to the Mumbai police and especially to Kushal's friend Pradeep Sharma. He decided to take revenge for his friend's murder at any cost. Sharma sent his entire team in search of Sadiq Kalia. They couldn't find his whereabouts but successfully got hold of his pager number. The Crime Branch kept the pager under surveillance. However, one day, the pager number went dead. An insider from the Crime Branch had switched sides and passed information to Shakeel about Kalia's pager being tracked. Kalia had then disconnected his pager.

But the Mumbai police were not about to give up so easily. They got the telecom company to activate the pager again. Subsequently, the subscriber received a message saying the pager company was offering a free trial for fifteen days. Kalia walked right into the trap set for him by the police. Kalia handed over the pager to his friend and accomplice, Chikna. They communicated over the pager, whereby Kalia would leave messages for Chikna from PCOs all over the city. But Kalia never waited at any of these spots for more than five minutes, making it impossible for the cops to track him down.

One day, Chikna received a message from Kalia, asking that he meet him at a cinema hall near Mumbai

Central. Chikna was surprised by the message, because Kalia had never asked to meet him in a crowded place before. The message had another recipient too—Sub-Inspector Daya Nayak who had kept the pager under surveillance. Nayak decided to take a chance and reached the cinema hall an hour earlier than the time decided between Chikna and Kalia. Daya parked his Maruti Zen at a distance from the theatre and waited.

After about ten minutes, a Yamaha motorcycle approached the cinema hall. The rider parked by the side and stood waiting. Daya got out of his car and started walking towards the bike. He quietly approached Chikna and jumped on the pillion seat in a quick movement. Daya pointed his gun at Chikna's back and asked him to get down immediately. A startled Chikna was horror-struck to see the inspector instead of his friend Kalia.

Other cops who were stationed nearby held Chikna down and took him away in a van. Kalia's most trusted accomplice was taken straight to the Crime Intelligence Unit. Next on the list was Kalia himself.

The Countdown Begins

The curled-up figure of a man sat in the corner of the special squad office. '*Saab jaane do na muje, Mai samjhaata na usko. Saab chod do na,*' Chikna pleaded with the cops. Instead, Daya slapped Chikna hard, right across his face. He caught Chikna by his collar and shook him with another loud slap on his head. '*Chal bol, Kalia kidhar milege? Kisko thokne ka plan tha?*' Daya growled.

Suddenly Chikna's pager beeped out loud. He had received a message which said, 'Dadar *phool* market at 4 p.m.' Daya smiled. He was now one step ahead of Sadiq Kalia. Daya got up and informed his senior about the turn of events. Inspector Pradeep Sharma jumped to his feet and in less than ten minutes he left his office with his team. Ten officers, including Daya, Arun Borude and a lady police officer, Sangeeta Patil, got into a car. Daya grabbed Chikna by his collar and shoved him in one of the cars. Chikna knew he was double-crossing his friend, but his own life was at stake and he had no option but to do as he was told. The cars then set out to finally take down the deadly killing machine, Sadiq Kalia.

December 12, 1997. It was a regular busy afternoon at the Dadar flower market. The place crackled with the chaos that was routine there. The grimy walls of the flyover housed an overflowing market right outside Dadar railway station. The narrow roads, parallel to the railway station, were filled with a crowd of vegetable vendors. The flower vendors were under the flyover, their baskets of flowers set out, ready for business. It was around 4 o'clock. The peak time for business for all. Commuters would swarm the markets at regular intervals, making their way through to the other side. Customers and sellers were busy bargaining over flowers, vegetables and fruits. Dadar phool market was the usual constant and unending pandemonium.

Amidst the bedlam of noise and hustle-bustle, a man stood stationary in a corner of the market, a cap hung low on his head. He watched people walking to and fro.

Suddenly, he showed signs of impatience. It seemed as though he was waiting for a friend who hadn't shown up. A man walked past him, throwing a dirty glance his way. The man, like everyone else at the market, was oblivious to the identity of the person in the cap—Sadiq Kalia.

The Bhoot was on a special mission this time. And without Chikna, the mission wouldn't be carried out. His next target was none other than Shiv Sena MP Mohan Rawle. The execution had been masterminded by Chhota Shakeel. He wanted Rawle dead to teach Arun Gawli a lesson. Despite his political background, Rawle's proximity to the Maharashtrian gangs was very evident. He had shown his solidarity with the Gawli gang and as well as his loyalty to the Naik gang. He had attended the funeral of gangster Amar Naik after he was killed in an encounter on 10 August 1996 and, in 1997, when Arun Gawli was booked under the National Security Act, Rawle had gone on a hungerstrike in protest for eight days outside the Agripada police station. He ended his fast only after Gawli's mother offered him a glass of juice. At his annual Dussehra speech at Shivaji Park, Bal Thackeray would routinely call the Maharashtrians among these mobsters '*amchi muley*'—'our boys'. And Rawle took pride in being associated with these sons of the soil.

Rawle was also a people-pleaser and wanted to be in everyone's good books. He took special care to not upset the sentiments of any particular gang, apart from Dawood's company, which he freely bad-mouthed. His political power was on the rise and his growing closeness to Arun Gawli was beginning to be a big threat to the D-Company. Arun Gawli's party, along with Rawle's support, were collectively becoming very powerful. Rawle's killing was supposed to serve as a warning to Gawli, and Sadiq Kalia had been chosen to execute the murder.

Sweat dropped from Kalia's forehead down onto his shirt. Time was running out and his partner and rider Chikna was nowhere to be seen. Kalia checked his pager again to see if he had missed a message from Chikna. There was nothing. Kalia let out a heavy sigh and looked around. He decided to wait for some more time.

'Bhago, Bhoot Aaya'

The two police teams reached the flower market around late afternoon. The huge crowds posed a problem to the police. Not only did they have to look for Kalia in the surge of people, but they also had to catch and arrest him. None of the officers had seen Kalia before and did not know what he looked like. But Sharma was determined to put an end to the gangster.

He decided not to stop his vehicle at the flower market, but instead asked his men to go ahead, take a U-turn and return. Daya went ahead in his car. He had Chikna captive with him, as he was the only person who could identify Kalia for them.

Chikna secretly hoped that Kalia would not be found at all. However at the same time his eyes kept scanning the crowd for his friend. Suddenly, Chikna spotted a man sporting a cap and staring into the distance. Chikna's eyes popped out in fear and he felt his stomach churn. It was Kalia, waiting impatiently for him. Daya saw Chikna's face change and guessed that he had seen what they had come looking for.

He followed Chikna's gaze and asked him, '*Kidhar hai vo?* Where is he?' Chikna remained silent.

Daya pulled out a revolver, calmly placed it at Chikna's forehead and said, '*Bol, nai toh idhar hi khol dunga*. Tell me, otherwise I will shoot you here itself.'

Chikna pointed a trembling hand towards Kalia. '*Saab vo laal topi wala. Vahi hai Kalia.* Sir, the man wearing a red hat. That is Kalia.' His voice quaked in fear.

Daya asked Chikna to identify him again. He did not want to take any chances. But Chikna was sure—it was Kalia. Daya alerted Sharma and the others who were in the other car. Sharma asked Daya to follow his vehicle. They reached the main road away from the market and took a U-turn. They then parked their cars near the station. One constable stayed back in one of the cars to watch Chikna. The other officers set out on foot towards Kalia.

Kalia could sense that something was wrong. His friend was late and his sharp eyes had noticed a certain white police cruiser circling the area twice. Then, he saw something that made his heart skip a beat. Sharma and his men were in clear sight and were headed his way. In the flash of a second, Kalia drew out two revolvers and opened fire at the police party. Kalia always had the habit of keeping two revolvers tucked into either side of his trousers. This was something he always pulled on everyone—shooting at a target with two guns.

The police had no way to save innocent civilians and yet not let Kalia get away. Suddenly, one of the constables came up with a juvenile but workable idea. He stood on the bonnet of a jeep and screamed, '*Bhago, bhoooooot aaya!* Run, a ghost has come!' This was the game-changer because people started running away, clearing the area for the police. Kalia felt cornered. The cops felt rejuvenated and it was time for them to show their heroics.

Kalia pelted bullets at the police who dodged them and took cover. Gunshots rang throughout the market, and people broke into a frantic stampede. Kalia knew he was surrounded by police on all sides and there was no option of escape. He lunged forward, hoping to take the police by surprise. Sharma and his team continued firing in his direction. The police had by then cleared the area of general public and Kalia couldn't use any civilian as cover. It had come down to a one-on-one fight. A duel between Sharma against Sadiq. Cop against criminal.

A lone Kalia was no match for a team of policemen. Sharma's men kept firing in his direction while Sharma crawled up to Kalia from behind his cover. He jumped on Kalia in a quick motion and kicked him down to his knees. Kalia dropped to the ground but he would not give up. Kalia rolled over, turning to fire at Sharma. Sharma already had a gun pointed at Kalia and he pulled the trigger. The other officers closed in and sprayed

Mumbai's most-wanted gangster with a series of bullets. Sadiq Kalia was finally dead. The man who had shaken the city with his gruesome acts of violence had finally been overpowered.

Sadiq Kalia's death went on to become one of the most famous encounters helmed by Pradeep Sharma and Daya Nayak together. However, Daya—who sustained a bullet injury in his thigh—was allowed to steal the limelight and hailed for his tenacity.

HITMAN 7
Boyhood to Bhaidom

Mumbai's Moharram

Barely five kilometres from southern Mumbai's elite business district lies Mohammed Ali Road, named after Mohammad Ali Jouhar who was an activist, scholar, journalist, poet and one of the presidents of the Indian National Congress for a short while in the early 1920s. Years later, no trace of Mohammed Ali's illustrious background or his vision can be seen anywhere in the vicinity of the Muslim borough.

The place is an urban nightmare, despite the intervention of a huge flyover called the J J Flyover that snakes its way through the southern tip of Mohammad Ali Road, beginning from the back of Crawford Market and winding its way 2.2 kms away to the state-run J J Hospital. It skips all the important landmarks of Mohammad Ali Road: J J Square, Iranian Masjid, Moghul Masjid, enclaves like Bohri Mohalla, the wonderful stalls and shops that sell henna, ittar, scarves, surmai, jewellery, lingerie, accessories, shoes, toys, books, Minara Masjid and Crawford Market junction. The flyover is so high that you will not even get a whiff of the food and delicacies served in the various bylanes of Mohammad Ali Road.

In that particular year, 1998, on May 6, there was no J J Flyover to mar the view of Mohammad Ali Road. It was the penultimate day of Muharram—Ashura. And Ashura is the day when Shia Muslims from all over Mumbai and its neighbouring districts descend to the east of J J Hospital all the way up to Imam Husain Chowk near Sandhurst Road railway station. It is a day to mourn Imam Hussain, the grandson of Prophet Mohammad, killed barbarically by a tyrannical ruler, Yazid, in the year 680 AD in Karbala, which is now in modern Iraq.

On that day, thousands of Shia Muslims had converged near J J Square, Dongri, Noor Baug, Mughal Masjid and its surrounding roads and were thumping their chests so hard that it felt like a thousand drums were beating as one for their beloved Imam Hussain in a show of grief and solidarity. Meanwhile, youngsters lashed themselves with chains and sharp knives that were freshly-sharpened.

The atmosphere rang with grieving elegies, self-flagellation and mournful ballads; red flags, youths and women dressed in black were part of the huge procession.

Conspiracy in Captivity

A stone's throw away, J J Hospital was going about their business as usual. The hospital, which has stood the test of time, is housed in a stone building constructed in 1845 by a philanthropic Parsi merchant, Jamshetjee Jeejebhoy, and the East India Company. It has been a mute witness to the social and cultural upheavals in the city and especially Mohammad Ali Road. It is now run by the Maharashtra state government to provide healthcare at subsidised costs to the economically poor from the entire south and southeastern fringes of Mumbai.

On that day, the hospital was as usual a hub of activity. The staff nurses were buzzing about and barking instructions to families crowding about patients. Just then, a team of six heavyset policemen walked into the hospital. The men were in khaki uniforms, and nestled between them was a lanky figure. His scrawny wrists were in handcuffs, and he tried to keep up with the policemen who roughly led him through the corridors of the hospital. Dressed in a loose, soiled shirt and dusty pants, the young boy looked very bright and intelligent. He had thick eyebrows and had a smart demeanour. His eyes had a happy smile and when he laughed, people were drawn to him. He was charm personified. He held his head high and his gaze was steady.

The boy was escorted to the second floor of the hospital and into the ward for prisoners. The boy was famished and a shrivelled shadow of his former self, so he did not evoke any fear in the nurse who was waiting for him. She, like many others, was oblivious to the identity of this twenty-one-year-old. 'What did you do?' the nurse asked.

'Amongst other things, I shot dead MLA Ramdas Nayak,' he replied, laughing.

The boy was Firoze Kokani after all: young, hot-blooded and the most dreaded sharpshooter of the underworld mafia.

Firoze scanned the corridors, looking for something. '*Sahab, time kya hua hai?*' he asked the constable, for the tenth time in the span of an hour.

'*Kyu be, bahot time puch raha hai, jo bhi ho tera toh bura time hi chal raha hai,* What, you're asking for the time so often; whatever time it is, it's a bad time for you,' the constable replied.

Firoze smirked at the constable and looked away, barely able to hide his eagerness for a certain visitor.

It was half past three now, and Firoze was scheduled to visit the radiology department for a CT scan. The police finally decided to take a break for their evening tea and left Firoze waiting outside the check-up ward. Firoze clasped his sweaty hands together, wondering what was taking his friend Sajid Batliwala so long.

The two had a tremendous bond—it was Sajid Batliwala who spotted Firoze's ferocity and decided to introduce him to the D-gang and Chhota Shakeel. When Firoze found out he would be taken to J J Hospital for a medical examination—despite being just twenty-one, he had a kidney ailment—he had immediately sent word to Sajid. The hospital was a place where the police's reins of power were often relaxed. They would often allow convicts to meet their relatives and lawyers either in the gardens or at the back of the hospital in return for some consideration. Two days prior to his examination, Sajid had sent his informer to meet Firoze in jail to pass on the plan detailing his escape.

Suddenly, Firoze heard a familiar voice. He lifted his face to see Sajid heading his way. Firoze's face lit up; the plan was in action. He grabbed Sajid's arm and pulled him to a corner. He asked Sajid what had taken him so long, and in hushed tones whispered quietly, '*Samaan laya kya?* Brought the stuff?' Sajid said nothing. Instead, he pulled out a black revolver from his pocket and thrust it into Firoze's hands. Firoze pulled his gaunt body into an upright posture. Sajid handed him another gun which Firoze quickly tucked into his shirt. He was no longer a helpless prey; he was now the predator.

Sajid motioned to Firoze that he would be waiting downstairs and left as quickly as he had come. It was time to turn the tables around.

Four guards returned from their tea break. They handcuffed Firoze again—they had been removed since he was in the radiology department—and pushed him forward towards the stairs. Ignorant of the impending disaster that awaited them, one of the guards poked Firoze with his baton to move faster down the steps. In a flash of a second, Firoze swiftly turned around and landed a heavy punch to the jaw of the guard. He pushed the guard down the stairs, pulled out his pistol and started firing. Gunshots resounded through the corridors, sending waves of horror and shock throughout the hospital. People were now running helter-skelter. Firoze took advantage of the commotion and started running towards the exit of the hospital. He may have shot down two guards, but he was still being chased by the other two. Firoze knew he had to get out of the hospital before they caught up with him. Handcuffed and panting, Firoze made his way through the frantic stampede that had ensued. He was quick as lightning.

In a flash, he made his way to the railings of the balcony on the first floor. Without a second thought, he climbed the railings and jumped to the ground floor. Firoze looked back at the two guards chasing him with their guns pointed in his direction. He lifted his own pistol and started firing in all directions. Then, limping, Firoze dragged himself to the gate. Outside, Sajid was waiting for Firoze on his motorbike. He spotted Firoze and kickstarted his bike. He rode his bike to Firoze and took a sharp turn at the gate. With a quick jump, Firoze got onto the bike and the duo sped off. Not only was Sajid skilled on the bike, but his speed was beyond match for most other riders.

Once out of sight of the hospital's gate, Firoze's handcuffs were removed. The duo put on black shirts and melted into the teeming crowds in the procession. The pulsating tempo of the chants of the procession matched the Firoze's heartbeats. He looked around at the crowds; nobody batted an eye in his direction. After having spent three years in jail, he was finally a free man.

This was one of the most audacious escapes scripted by a member of the Mumbai underworld. Firoze's escape left the Mumbai police redfaced. To let a convict of Firoze's notoriety escape from under their noses left a deep stain on their reputation. One of the constables guarding him, B. D. Kardile, had even lost his life.

To begin with, the elusive gunman had only been

arrested after months of pursuit by then deputy commissioner of police, crime, Rakesh Maria. Had it not been for Maria's perseverance, the police would never have managed to lay their hands on Firoze. Maria's team had successfully nabbed and arrested Firoze in Bangalore, and the feat was considered a major success for the team.

'I had warned everyone that Firoze would get away. We had internal information about a plan, and the information was forwarded to the men,' stated Rakesh Maria, now director-general of the home guards.

Firoze and Sajid finally reached Reti Bandar at Kalwa, near Thane. They abandoned the bike and went their separate ways. The man behind the cold-blooded murder of BJP MLA Ramdas Nayak was free. Ten days later, Firoze Kokani headed to Dubai, never to be seen or heard of again.

A Date with Death

Around the end of 1993, BJP leader Ramdas Nayak had just emerged as a power force like no other political figure. He had a dour persona but was a smart politician. His clout was huge. Nayak was best known for his twelve-year private legal battle over the cement scandal that forced A. R. Antulay to step down as the state's chief minister. The buzz was that Ramdas Nayak would bag the chief minister's chair if the BJP came to power, and the chances of the BJP–Shiv Sena coalition coming to power was strong at the time (eventually the Shiv Sena rode to power in 1995 and with them the BJP). Who gave the *supari* for Ramdas Nayak's killing will always remain a mystery. Was it somebody in the BJP itself? Was it the Congress? Was it a financial deal gone wrong? Everybody was a suspect. While competing politicians within the BJP had reason to bump him off, so did the Opposition parties, as they had seen his dogged determination resulting in the rout of Congress heavyweight Antulay. Nayak was a real threat and a dangerous opponent.

The killing contract was bagged by D-Company's ganglord Chhota Shakeel. And Chhota Shakeel in all his wisdom thought it fit to assign the job to one of his more recent finds; someone he had discovered two years earlier during the communal riots that rocked Mumbai.

It was a usual busy day at Hill Road, Bandra. The street was bustling with vendors and people moving around in swarms. Following Nayak for the fifth consecutive day were Firoze and Sajid Batliwala. The two made a great team: Sajid had discovered the raw talent in Firoze and thought he was perfect for the job of a hitman. If Firoze had channelized his energies elsewhere, he would have succeeded. The kid was bright and had a lot of promise.

Firoze and Sajid knew that killing Nayak was not going to be easy. The BJP leader was heavily protected by armed bodyguards at all times. They would need far more sophisticated weapons than the ones Nayak's guards were armed with. But as the famous adage goes among cops and criminals, it is the machine that matters as much as the man who manages it. The guts of the gunman is always more crucial than the gears of the gun.

To say that Firoze was adept with a gun was an understatement. The twenty-one-year-old was known to have the skills to successfully shoot his targets in total darkness. A gun was his favorite toy and Sajid trusted his aim. It was thus decided that Firoze would take the shot. This was one of the most prestigious killing contracts, and they could not afford a mistake. They practiced dummy runs of the killing in secluded places. Sajid trained Firoze on how to use an AK-47.

On 25 August 1994, the duo woke up in the wee hours of the morning. It is said that, for any gunman, the morning of an execution requires gallons of gall to move. When it was broad daylight, Sajid Batliwala and Firoze Kokani set out, loaded with guns and about to assassinate one of the city's top political leaders. One of the hardest contractual killings had been assigned to them and needed to be finished.

Around nine o'clock in the morning, Nayak stepped out of his Bandra residence and got into his Ambassador car. He took the back seat, with his personal and police guard in the front. The car approached the main road and took a turn towards S. V. Road. It slowed down in the traffic and stopped at a signal. Firoze and Sajid were already stationed near the signal. They spotted Nayak's car and approached it quickly, not together but from opposite sides. Sajid began shooting randomly to divert the bodyguard's attention towards himself and distract everyone.

Before Nayak could figure out what was happening, Firoze fired a volley of bullets at the vehicle. Nayak's police guard pulled out his sten gun, but it was no match for Firoze's AK-47. He put up a great fight, but lost his life in the battle along with Ramdas Nayak. Firoze informed his men, who had been posted near Nayak's residence in case the politician surived the attack and returned home, to run. The men hijacked an auto on the way and threatened the driver at gunpoint to speed off. The other men stationed close by escaped in a Fiat and on bikes.

Both Nayak and his guard were rushed to a nearby hospital but they were declared dead on admission. Nayak's private guard survived the gunfight.

The Fugitive Firoze

As soon as news of Nayak's killing broke out, the political scene heated up with the BJP insisting that the murder was a result of political rivalry. The Mumbai police groped in the dark to find a motive that would lead them to the murderer. It was suspected that this was a supari killing, given the attack was carried out with a weapon of such tremendous firepower. The last time an AK-47 was used in Mumbai was in a shootout at the state-run J J Hospital in September 1992. The police team, led by DCP Rakesh Maria, investigated a number of angles. Besides a land dispute and an underworld contract killing, other theories included Afghan mercenaries from Kashmir who wanted revenge against Nayak for helping to fight terrorism in Doda.

The police department were particularly keen to find

out who was behind the shootout as one of their own was killed in the attack. In the '80s and '90s, police informers were very active. These shadowy figures lived on the threshold of death as they were constantly dallying with both the police and the mafia. Inspector Dinesh Kadam from Maria's team had a good network of informants and Maria lost no time in putting them to work now. Soon enough, he found out that it was Firoze who had carried out the shootout. He then put his best men on Firoze's trail to track him. But for a year, there was no sign of Firoze or any of his accomplices.

The cops got their first clue in October the following year. An informer alerted Sub-Inspector Dinesh Kadam that Firoze had been seen in Bangalore, where he was going to carry out his next assignment. Kadam immediately left with his men and stayed put near Hotel Blue Diamond, where Firoze and two others were holed up. The cops first confirmed his presence in the hotel and decided to arrest him in the night so that other patrons would not be disturbed. But they were faced with one major setback. Nobody knew what Firoze Kokani looked like. The only thing they knew about him was that he wore an earring in his left ear. It was a risky ambush for the Mumbai police, and that too on alien turf.

Around midnight, Kadam and his officers went to the second floor of the hotel. They went up to the Firoze's room and, to their surprise, saw that the door was ajar. One of them knocked on the door, and when nobody answered, they gave it a slight push. When the door swung open, the cops saw a man sipping a drink, sitting alone in the room. The police found out later that the two other men who had been with Firoze had gone to see a *mujra* show, and Firoze had decided to stay back alone. He had left his door open, thinking that his men would return soon and he wanted to have his drinks undisturbed.

As soon as Firoze saw the cops enter, he made a mad dash towards the bed where he had stocked his weapons. However, Kadam and his men kicked Firoze down with one hard blow and pushed him to the ground. He was quickly overpowered and cornered. The police sat him down on the sofa, and whipped him to start him talking. During the interrogation, Firoze confessed to the Ramdas Nayak killing and revealed his other partners in the crime.

'Firoze was cornered with no support; he had no chance of an escape. He had to submit,' concluded Kadam.

The fact that Kadam and his forces had nabbed Firoze was not disclosed. It was a crucial time and while his capture was kept a secret, Kadam was able to coax names and addresses of other members of the gang from Firoze. The information was then passed to the police. The forces dispatched a search party to all the hotels and places where the others were hiding.

The usual operandi was as follows. The police party would reach a particular hotel and confirm to Kadam that the accused were in one of the rooms. Firoze was then made to call the accused and inform them of a police crackdown. Firoze was made to tell him that an associate was already arrested and they were next. Kadam had instructed his officers to be stationed downstairs in civil clothes and when the accused would exit the hotel in a hurry, they would be arrested. The fact that they were rushing out of the hotel was their identification.

'We arrested at least five men in a similar way. The cops knew that the person running away from the hotel would be an accused. Nobody else would leave their hotel rooms in such panic at two in the morning,' said Kadam.

One by one, all the men accused in the Ramdas Nayak murder were nabbed by the cops. This was a major success for the police force. However it was shortlived. Three years later, Firoze Kokani, the main accused in the murder, successfully staged a daring escape.

During the course of the investigation conducted afterwards, it was learnt that Kokani's father Abdullah had plotted his escape. He and two cops, Sub-Inspector Satish Gawte and Constable Surya Sawant, were later arrested by the police for aiding and abetting Kokani's escape.

The Making of a Killer

After the serial blasts of 1993 and towards the beginning of 1994, underworld kingpin and don Dawood Ibrahim left Dubai and relocated to Karachi. His ace lieutenant Chhota Shakeel began to expand his network in Mumbai. Shakeel would recruit Muslim boys in their early teens to his gang and groom them to shoot and kill. Most of these boys were school dropouts and had a fascination for the gang culture. They were hot-blooded and thrived on the idea of becoming a 'bhai'. Also, they came from lower middle class families and would do anything for money. It was an era when gangs were heralded as the hub where one could make pots of money and every boy wanted his share of cash and the glory that came with the association. For these young boys, pulling a trigger for a sum of five thousand rupees meant nothing more than a challenge.

One such boy who caught Shakeel's eye in particular was Firoze Sarguroh.

Firoze Abdullah Sarguroh alias Firoze Kokani had committed his first crime at the age of 16. He hailed from a conservative Muslim family of four children who lived in the Shaikh Mistry Dargah area of Antop Hill. Firoze had a sister and a brother elder to him and a younger brother. While his brothers and sisters did well in school and college, Firoze was a class nine drop out.

He grew up with boys in Dongri in South Mumbai- the hub of Mumbai's Muslim Mafiosi- where he used to moonlight as an office boy in an export office at Nishanpada Road. Bad company and the lure of an easy life led him to his first crime in 1992 when he along with his cronies assaulted a drunkard outside a liquor joint and made away with his watch and wallet. The man succumbed to his injuries the next day.

This murder ensured that he gained notoriety as a dada and the shopkeepers and businessmen in South Mumbai, Pydhonie, Nagpada and Madanpura began dreading his visits. Impressed, a builder offered him a job of a bodyguard. He was a haggard 17 year old > He did his job well –braking bones and smashing cars when needed. He also hung around the Maharashtra College looking for good looking girls. He shot I nto the big league after two incidents—a contract for attacking Syed Mannan, a crime branch informer and beating up Chota Shakeel men when they approached his builder boss for protection money.

But few know that Firoze was instrumental in the second round of communal riots that hit Mumbai in 1993. In January 1993, Firoxe had cold-bloodedly stabbed two Mathadi workers to death in the Masjid Bunder area.

In his teens, young Firoze had cold-bloodedly stabbed two Mathadi workers to death in the Masjid Bunder area in January 1993.

The breakout of communal riots in Mumbai after the demolition of the Babri Masjid on 6 December 1992 had changed the character of the city. On 6 January 1993, several cases of stabbing were reported in areas like Dongri, Pydhonie, V. P. Road and Nagpada jurisdictions in south Mumbai. All these spots were in the vicinity of Mohammad Ali Road.

Death and panic danced on the streets of Mumbai as the city witnessed some of the worst riots in its history. Cases of stabbing, arson, mob violence and attacks on private and government properties occurred in Dongri, Pydhonie, V. P. Road, Nagpada, Tardeo, Mahim,

Dharavi, Nirmal Nagar, Chembur and Kherwadi. Most of the stabbing cases occurred in isolated lanes and bylanes, and by the time the police would arrive at the scene, the miscreants would have vanished. Mob violence accounted for the deaths of many innocent people.

Firoze Sarguroh had just stepped into adolescence then. He had grown up in Antop Hill, not very far from Mohammad Ali Road. And like many other youngsters, he was deeply scarred by the communal tension blazing through the city. He took to the streets to avenge the atrocities committed against his fellow Muslim brothers. Looting, arson, torching police vehicles were acts of revenge he happily indulged in. He and his friends had taken it upon themselves to bring justice to their Muslim brothers who were slaughtered during the riots.

Though mob violence and instigation by various political parties further fuelled the riots, a lot of damage was also done by rumours. Rumours of a large number of people of a particular community being killed created an air of intense panic and commotion, causing people to either retreat into hiding, or pick up their swords. Amidst the riots, there were also several stabbing incidents which were carried out by professional criminals. And such incidents were being reported in different areas of the city. It appeared that someone was doing this with the explicit intention to increase communal tensions, especially during the first phase of the riots in December 1992. Most of the victims stabbed by these professional criminals were Hindus. It appeared that these stabbings were part of an organized plan by killers at the behest of unknown sources. But given that all the victims were

Hindus, it was a clear that the people behind them were Muslims.

The Muslim criminal elements operating in south Bombay included people like Salim Rampuri and they were ultimately identified as the brains behind the stabbing incidents. Hindus used this to further fuel the fire. On 1 January 1993, Bal Thackeray, in his mouthpiece *Saamna,* wrote *'Hindunni akramak vhayala have'* (Hindus ave to become more aggressive). The next day a number of Muslim hutments in the compound of M. P. Mill in Tardeo were set on fire. On the same day, there was an incident in Dharavi where two Muslims were assaulted with iron rods. Again, on 3 January 1993, a Muslim in Dharavi jurisdiction was attacked with a knife. Muslim settlements were singled out and surveys were conducted by the Shiv Sainiks. In Asalpha in Ghatkopar, a taxi ferrying a Muslim family, including a bearded man and a burqa-clad woman with two children, was set ablaze.

Seventeen-year-old Firoze Sarguroh was not a very tolerant boy. The growing number of attacks against his community pushed him to pick up his own weapons. As per his own confession to the police, on one night he saw a news capsule called *Ghumta Aaina* (The Revolving Mirror), which showed atrocities on Muslims across the country. Firoze was disturbed by the news reports and images.

He decided to target Hindus where it would hurt the most. The Mathadi workers who lifted huge weights in the docks and other parts of Mumbai were a strong power force in themselves. Though they were not aligned to any right-wing Hindu parties, they were Hindus. Consequently, an attack on a Mathadi worker would be an attack on Hindus. Also, because he lived in a locality which neighboured the Mathadi workers' settlements, they were convenient targets.

Night had just fallen on 5 January 1993. A fog of fear blanketed the city. The grisly silence of the night was about to be broken. Firoze had been keeping a watch on the godown of a transport company in south Mumbai. He had stationed himself behind a truck so nobody would see him. A Mathadi worker who was sleeping in the go-down dragged his sleepy self across the street to relieve himself. Firoze followed him, and before the Mathadi worker could anticipate his fate, Firoze attacked him from behind and stabbed him to death. His screams alerted three other Mathadi workers who rushed to the scene. But they were no match for a raging Firoze, who took both of them down with his knife. The frenzied assault resulted in the death of two men, while two were left injured and bleeding.

The murders of the Mathadi workers lit up Mumbai in new flames of communal tension.

The Mathadi Workers' Union called for a bandh the next day and meetings were held. The public, like the police, were oblivious to the identity of the man behind the killings. The Shiv Sena openly accused Muslims of being responsible for the ruthless murders, thus instigating another round of 'an eye for an eye' revenge.

Two days later, a mob of Hindu people attacked

Muslims in Mahim. This led to the second phase of the riots, only more brutal and gruesome this time. Firoze was thus single-handedly responsible for engineering the second round of riots in the city.

Don Dumps Darling

After having recruited Firoze, Chhota Shakeel developed a close bond with the young shooter. They shared a rapport so strong that often Shakeel addressed Firoze with all kinds of endearing names, which was quite unusual behaviour for a gangster of his stature. Shakeel and Firoze would call each other 'Darling', something that the don did not do with any of his other gang members.

Under the tutelage of Chhota Shakeel, Firoze Kokani became a hardened killer. He killed an innocent Shaikh Hanif Patel by mistake when he was targeting a Shiv Sena leader Raghunath Sagwekar. He killed Ashfaq Koorla at Pune, fired at Rahim in Null Bazaar, shot at builder Bhagat and killed one person in Vikhroli. He depleted the crime branch' sources of information by killing several informers. He shot dead Tasleem Ghare at Dongri, Haji Bidar, an erstwhile partner of narco-don, Mohammad Dosssa and Praveen Zubair at Crawford Market.

Soon after his escape from J J Hospital, Firoze crossed over to Nepal through the porous border and reached Dubai. From there, it was easy to unite with his boss in Karachi. But when Firoze landed in Karachi, his ambitions had grown manifold. He desired the throne for himself. Firoze thought Shakeel was a small-town guy who had just gotten lucky, and that he, Firoze, had undertaken many risky assignments and killings and had made a prominent name for himself. He thought it was time to dethrone Shakeel. But Firoze had overlooked the fact that his utility in Shakeel's gang was that of a shooter. Firoze lacked the leadership skills of a boss. And Shakeel would never concede his power and glory to any man.

Later it was revealed that Dawood Ibrahim's brother, Anis Ibrahim, was not happy with Firoze, as he had discovered that he was backbiting him. Somebody had taped a conversation in which Firoze was recorded liberally abusing Anis. This proved fatal for Firoze.

Firoze failed to understand the basic principles and protocols of hierarchy in the D-Company, and the result was that somebody plotted to have him eliminated from the scene. Shakeel made an agreement with the Mumbai police to hand over Firoze Kokani in exchange for amnesty for his gang. The story goes that Firoze was then nabbed in a market in Karachi in 2003, based on a tip-off from none other than his own boss and leader. The way to get power is to grab it, but Firoze Kokani was no match for Chhota Shakeel or Anis Ibrahim and thus came an abrupt end to the scintillating stories of the twenty-one-year-old shooter.

The theory is that, if he were alive, Firoze Kokani would have continued with his trail-blazing career in the mafia. Only his death could have put paid to his plans. His friend Sajid Batliwala also escaped with him to Dubai and Pakistan but returned to India three years later. The law caught up with him after twelve years when he made a couple of mistakes with his new identity whilst living in Mira Road, a suburb of Mumbai.

Among all the mafia boys, the story of Firoze Abdullah Sarguroh alias Firoze Kokani is an especially sad one. Here was a promising young lad, very intelligent, good-looking, smart, an absolute charmer who simply took the wrong path. At the age of seventeen he had committed his first murder, and by twenty-one he was an old hand with eighteen murders behind him, and scores of robberies, stabbing and firing cases. At one point of time he was regarded as the youngest and most ferocious killing machine in the Dawood gang.

The boy was actually a victim of both the mafia and political parties. The way he sprayed Ramdas Nayak with his AK-47, without any fear of Nayak's bodyguard retaliating, has been pointed out. And the very fact that most of the murders committed by Firoze Kokani were politicians—including Shiv Sena leaders R. T. Sagwekar and Vilas Sawant—seems to indicate that the mafia and politicians used the boy, and then disposed of him when he was of no use to them.

And it is not that Kokani got his dues from the mafia. It is said that, in 1998, when Kokani was taken by Batliwala to meet Dawood Ibrahim in Karachi, the don did not like Kokani's attitude at all. Firoze was gauche, as he was very young, and boasted of his murders and achievements. Batliwala had to apologize to Dawood for his temerity in bringing the young impudent lad to meet a don of his stature.

Whatever Dawood thought of the boy's boasting, the truth is that some of Kokani's actions had a great impact. For instance, in the way that the riots took on a different hue after the Mathadi workers were stabbed by him. To this day, Mumbai sits on a communal tinderbox and the scars have not healed. Ramdas Nayak was very likely to have become the chief minister of Maharashtra, as he was steadily climbing the ladder in the BJP hierarchy. Firoze Kokani changed both the political fortunes of a party and the state by cutting Ramdas Nayak from the fray. Firoze Kokani's life was a short one, but the mayhem he unleashed changed Mumbai's history.

HITMAN 8

From Political Assassin to Padre

The Target and the Threat

'*Nanga kardoonga*!!'

The furious threat reverberated throughout the sixth floor of Mantralaya, the seat of the Maharashtra government's administration, causing everyone to look up from what they were doing.

The bearded old man wearing a kurta pyjama seemed to be infuriated about something. He was trembling with rage and fury.

The man was a regular visitor to Mantralaya and was known to the administrative staff on the sixth floor, which only housed the offices of the chief minister and the home minister of the state. This corridor of power was not easily accessible even to several ministers. But Maulana Ziauddin Bukhari, former Member of Legislative Assembly (MLA) from the Muslim League, was a man who could not be stopped by red tape or bureaucratic screening. He was known to barge into offices, meetings and closed-door deliberations, and was thus a familiar face to officers and clerks.

During the intense and violent bout of riots in Antop Hill and Sion area, when hundreds of Muslims were trapped and unable to step out for fear of being killed by Shiv Sainiks on a rampage, Bukhari had rescued hordes of terrified people with the help of army trucks.

Bukhari was well-known in Muslim circles in the city and had tremendous clout. Considered to be a powerful orator, Bukhari's vitriolic speeches held lakh-strong audiences enthralled during his sermons in congregational Eid Namaz in Azad Maidan in south Mumbai. Bukhari's strident virulence and aggression had endeared him to the community and put fear in the hearts of his detractors. He was emerging as a strong Muslim leader and the community looked up to him.

It helped that Bukhari was also a shrewd businessman. He had managed to procure a huge piece of land in the prime locality of Oshiwara in Andheri West and built twenty-nine buildings between 1970 and 1980. Millat Nagar, as it's called, is nowan exclusive colony inhabited largely by Muslims.

It was this pull and connection with the community that no politician in his right mind could ignore.

Since 12 March 1993, when the city was rocked by serial bomb blasts resulting in the deaths of over 257 people and injury to over 800, Bukhari had been helping the government with investigations and playing the role of mediator between the community and politicians.

But today, despite several weeks of dedicated and diligent service for the government, Bukhari felt humiliated. Apparently, the chief minister, Sharad Pawar, had refused to meet him, which had enraged Bukhari. Instead of calmly leaving, the man had exploded in fury and issued loaded and dangerous threats.

'They don't know who they are crossing. They don't know! I will expose all of them,' he shouted, as his aide cowered in fear.

'I will call a bloody press conference and tell everyone who is really behind the 1992 riots, the killer of Muslims, and who is behind the March 1993 blasts and the massacre of Hindus,' he went on. '*Mujhse jang bahot mehengi saabit hogi. Nanga karke rakh doonga ek ekko!*' Bukhari thundered. All fingers pointed towards a particular minister in the Congress government.

The threat was heard by many and assimilated with varying reactions. While some were left wondering, others speculated.

One mind in particular was thinking very hard. Bukhari needed to be silenced. The state government could not afford a controversy now. If Bukhari managed to stir the hornet's nest, then it could topple the government. The minister's mind began working deviously.

Those who knew Bukhari well knew his shady and indelible past. Bukhari had risen to power with the support of Bashu Dada, one of the original dons of the city. Long before the flashier generation of gangsters like Dawood Ibrahim Kaskar, Chhota Rajan and Arun Gawli, there was Bashu Dada, a burly, fearsome ganglord who ran an *akhada*, wrestling ring, in Teli Mohalla and ruled Dongri with an iron fist. Dada would always be seen with heavy-set, menacing bodyguards flanking him, and no one dared to cross his path.

With Bashu Dada's support, Bukhari entered politics and went on to rise through the ranks till he became an MLA. However, his election was set aside by the Bombay High Court since he had used communal speeches to win the election. After Bashu's death, Bukhari became close to Haji Mastan and Dawood Ibrahim. During his ascent through the state's political hierarchy, he also developed close ties with the then chief minister, Sharad Pawar.

Now, on that scorching April afternoon in 1993, all the people who heard Bukhari's threats eagerly waited to see what would happen next. They expected something drastic to unfold, something that would shake the government and expose certain ministers and their involvement in the recent blasts. Something dramatic did happen. But it was not what anyone had anticipated.

The Supari

While other ganglords in the city were on the run and had left the country, Gawli had preferred to stay put and control his boys. Now, Gawli's fortress, Dagdi Chawl, in Byculla, was shrouded in a strange silence. The gang had just been offered the *supari* of a highly-respected Muslim leader. Gawli was loath to accept the contract. Despite being a devout Hindu, Gawli had married a Muslim woman, Zubeida Mujawar, from Wadgaon Pir in Pune. He did not want to be known as a Muslim baiter. Killing a Muslim gangster was justifiable, but how would he explain the killing of a venerable maulana? On the other hand, Gawli could not refuse the supari as it had come from a top politician in the Maharashtra government, who was also a Union Cabinet minister in the Congress regime, as well as a close friend of his arch enemy Dawood Ibrahim. He wanted nothing to do with Dawood, and if he took the supari, he would be indirectly helping Dawood, he thought. *Why didn't the strongman go to Dawood and his cronies instead of putting me in this dilemma?* Gawli wondered.

Besides, Gawli also had a paucity of shooters who would dare to step into a Muslim locality and fire at a respected priest and stage a safe escape. Bipin Shere and Shailesh Haldankar had shot dead Dawood Ibrahim's brother-in-law Ibrahim Parkar at Nagpada in July 1992 and were almost lynched by bystanders. Killing Bukhari would be equally tricky.

Gawli could only trust two of his men at that moment, Sada Pawle and Raju Shirsat Philips. Finally Raju solved Gawli's problem by accepting the gauntlet. Gawli was relieved.

Bukhari's office was below the Byculla Bridge near Khada Parsi Chowk. It was a predominantly Muslim locality. The hitman was expected to kill the man and ensure that he was back in the cocoon of Dagdi Chawl—which was barely 1,500 metres away from Bukhari's office—before the neighbourhood erupted in reaction.

On the morning of 21 April 1993, Bukhari had just stepped into his office when two men entered it. Their intrusion, lack of customary greetings, total disregard for any decorum, was shocking. Before Bukhari or his companions could make a move, one of them whipped out a gun, fired several rounds at him at point blank range, and both men fled. Bukhari died on the spot.

There was shock at this ruthless murder. And with the shock came anger. And with the anger came furious cries for justice and the usual accusations that the police were just mute bystanders and useless. The Mumbai police, anticipating a severe backlash the moment the murder was reported to them, had in fact swung into action, tapping sources, picking up suspects and doing everything else they could to track the killers.

The speculation was that this was the handiwork of the D-Company. At the time, Dawood had already fled to Dubai and was running his gang from there. He was the first choice for contract killings: he had a wide array of shooters at his disposal, men who were ready to further themselves in his good books by adding another feather to their caps, or more suitably, another scalp to their belts.

A month of intensive inquiries with all known Dawood aides in the city yielded nothing in terms of clues, leaving the police flummoxed. If anything, Dawood's men themselves appeared to be clueless about who had taken such a big supari. Bukhari was a hugely-famous Muslim leader with a wide following, and it took guts to accept a hit on someone like him. More importantly, they were curious to know who had dared to accept and execute a contract in the city that they thought they ruled.

The answer, when it came, stumped policemen and criminals alike. Bukhari had not been killed by the Dawood gang. It was, in fact, the Arun Gawli gang that had executed the contract.

Even more surprising, though, was the shooter.

Short, scrawny and bespectacled, Raju Philips walked with a slight limp and went against every stereotype that existed of a dreaded killer. Nondescript, diminutive and timid-looking, no one could believe that Raju Shirsat, alias Philips, was the contract killer who had shot Bukhari. This four-and-a-half foot man had stunned the underworld and the city with the way he had coolly entered Bukhari's office and shot him dead.

According to the treatise compiled by then joint commissioner of police, crime, M. N. Singh, tentatively titled, 'The Growth of Gangsterism in Mumbai', Philips was the third senior-most leader in the Gawli gang, and in charge of extortion and gang activities in the Byculla area.

Meeting Bukhari's Killer

Peon Chawl is a building a few metres from the Byculla station on the eastern side. The building is part of a cluster of buildings, each comprising long corridors of single-room tenements. At the time, most of the residents of the building were lower middle class Maharashtrian labourers, including mill workers.

Since the building is close to Dagdi Chawl and houses several Gawli loyalists, not many crime journalists venture to the area, let alone enter the building asking for the room of Raju Philips.

But then, Hussain Zaidi didn't fit the stereotype. He asked me to accompany him to Raju's house—he was working on a story and he needed Raju's inputs. In case things went awry and Raju decided to kill him, at least I could inform the police and Hussain's family, he said. I found the proposition to be quite risky and reckless, but tagged along with him.

Raju turned out be unexpectedly warm and friendly. Hussain's apprehensions were unfounded. Raju introduced us to his cheerful, smiling wife. We saw Christian symbols—a crucifix, a picture of the Madonna, a Bible—all over the place. Perhaps Raju had converted to Christianity after marrying the love of his life, herself a Christian. Raju could not walk without the help of a walking stick.

Raju offered us soft drinks and coffee, but Zaidi bluntly and undiplomatically refused. Raju thought it was because of his dubious profession. He said, 'I will ask my wife to make some tea for you.' But Hussain refused to have tea as well; it was one of his principles: to not break bread with either the mafia or the police.

We discussed a lot of things with Raju. We found out that he had faced a lot of atrocities after he was booked under the Terrorist and Disruptive Activities (TADA) Act following Bukhari's killing.

This was a time when the rivalry between Gawli and Ashwin Naik was at its peak, despite both of them being Maharashtrians. When Hussain brought up their rivalry,

Raju became agitated. His small frame was full of fury.

'*Sab bolneki baatein hain* (It's just talk),' Raju told us. 'The truth is that the police are on the payroll of all our rivals, and their sole mission is to eliminate us. Only our men are killed in encounters. Others are arrested or allowed to flee the country.' The Shiv Sena only supported Amar Naik (Amar Naik was eventually killed and Ashwin Naik, Amar Naik's younger brother, heads his gang now) because his sister-in-law Neeta Naik was in their party; they had no sympathy for Daddy (Gawli), Raju insisted.

Hussain continued to visit Raju on and off. Once, he found Raju at the sewing machine, trying to stitch clothes. The gangster was struggling with the machine because it required both feet to work it, and his bad foot was not efficient in its movements. Hussain also tried to get Raju to introduce him to another hitman from the Gawli gang—the strangely named Paul Newman. But Raju refused to set up a meeting.

Once, the British author Misha Glenny visited Mumbai for research on his book on organized gangs. He asked Hussain for help in this, and they would frequently meet at the Persian Darbar restaurant at Byculla for lunch and dinner. When Misha requested Hussain to get the Crime Branch's dossier on the Arun Gawli gang for his research, Hussain managed to do so. Misha acknowledged Hussain's help in his international bestseller on world gangs, *McMafia*.

Misha almost jumped out of his seat when he found the mention of Paul Newman's name in the list.

'I thought Paul Newman was a top actor in Hollywood movies; why is his name mentioned among the sharpshooters of the Gawli gang?' Misha could not hide his chagrin.

We explained to him that it was a just a coincidence. Misha said perhaps Paul's parents were a big fan of the Hollywood star and they had named him after the actor. However, the baffled look on Misha's face still amuses us whenever we talk about the incident.

Philips as Politician

Philips, one of the two Christian members in Gawli's gang, was born in Peon Chawl in Byculla and was recruited into the gang at a young age. He participated in several extortion jobs for Gawli, picking up targets from their residences or offices and taking them to Dagdi Chawl. Here, they would be made to sit in a corner for a couple of hours, listening to Gawli's thugs talk about murdering or maiming someone or the other. The cowering targets would then be taken to Gawli, where the ganglord would demand money from them. The slightest sign of defiance would elicit a trip to the dreaded 'inquiry room', where targets were beaten mercilessly by the likes of Sada Pawle, a particularly cruel Gawli aide. Any resistance would quickly disappear and the target would put all his remaining energy into arranging for the sum that Gawli had demanded.

Bukhari's murder thrust Philips into the limelight, turning him overnight from just another Gawli man to a name to be taken seriously. Gawli himself was in the Yerawada central jail at the time, having been arrested under the Terrorist and Disruptive Activities (TADA) Act, but he had quickly worked out a way of running the gang from inside the jail. It was just a matter of greasing the right palms, which Gawli did, and in no time orders were being issued from inside the jail, and Sada Pawle, in whose hands the reins fell in Gawli's absence, took care to enforce them.

Philips, after his involvement in the murder was revealed, became one of the most wanted men at the time. He was arrested a month after the murder, but he had by this time become immune to the police's interrogation techniques, his strong resentment for the cops having turned into a suit of armour.

Philips' hatred for anything khaki was connected to his limp. Philips was born with perfectly healthy legs. However, in the early '90s, he was picked up in connection with one of the scores of extortion cases against Gawli. His unflinching loyalty towards Daddy sealed his lips and he refused to open his mouth, no matter how much he was pressurized. The loyalty, however, came with a price. He was subjected to such intensive third-degree methods that he sustained a fracture to his right leg. The policemen who had picked him up did not provide medical aid in time, perhaps to avoid action for inhuman interrogation methods, and when Philips walked out of the lock-up, he had a permanent limp, as the fracture never healed properly.

A photograph taken at a party in Dagdi Chawl a day

before Philips was picked up by the police shows him dancing merrily with other Gawli aides, a smile on his face, without a care in the world. Little did Philips know that he would never dance again. At least not without grimacing in pain each time he put his right leg to the ground.

From that day onwards, each limping step that Philips took reminded him of the fact that the men in khaki were no better than the criminals that he hobnobbed with on a daily basis. His hatred and disdain for the police was visible and intense.

After securing bail in the Bukhari murder case, Philips went back to the Dagdi Chawl as a celebrity. He was now in the big league and, apart from being sent on more and more extortion and murder jobs, he was also given a prominent place in the Akhil Bharatiya Sena (ABS), the political party that Gawli had founded.

Gawli made Philips the spokesperson for the party, and Philips used his position to launch scathing attacks against the police force, calling them corrupt, inefficient and biased, and dismissing their encounter specialists as little more than hitmen in uniform for rival gangs.

His loyalty to Gawli also manifested itself in violent ways, and he was among the first to attack anyone who said a word against Daddy. Anindita Ramaswamy, a journalist with the *Asian Age*, was one such victim. In 1997, she published an article in the daily saying that Gawli, who was still in jail at the time, was facing problems in paying his gang members regularly, which could impact his image and sway on the city's underworld. Needless to say, the article did not go down very well with either Gawli or his trusted aides. The ABS was at the time trying to gather as much clout as possible to contest the upcoming parliamentary elections in 1999. It had faced humiliating defeats in the previous elections, with twelve of its candidates, including Philips himself, having to forfeit their deposit. Philips and another Gawli hitman Sunil Ghate had contested the corporation election and lost. The jeers of '*zamaanat zapt*', 'lost his deposit', still echoed in their ears and the article only angered them further.

Ramaswamy went to Dagdi Chawl the same day that the article was published to do a follow-up story. While she was making her inquiries in the chawl, a Gawli aide came up to her and asked her who she was. Dagdi Chawl, although teeming with armed and mean-looking thugs working for Gawli, was usually open to journalists. Philips himself met and interacted with a lot of reporters to try and further the image of Gawli as a poor, helpless soul being targeted by the police, as well as to gain political mileage for the ABS. Nevertheless, the gang members made it their business to closely monitor the interactions of journalists in the chawl.

On hearing that she was a journalist with the *Asian Age*, the henchman told Ramaswamy that the article on Gawli had been read that morning and that the one responsible would not be spared. Ramaswamy told him that she was just looking for information on an ABS office in Dadar, and he told her to wait. She then exited the chawl and informed her office about what had happened. But instead of leaving the scene, she bravely went back inside and waited where the man had told her to.

Meanwhile, the Gawli henchman ran to Philips and told him that the journalist responsible for the article about Daddy was at this moment inside Dagdi Chawl. A furious Philips rounded up a small team and left for the spot immediately.

Ramaswamy had only just come back to the spot after calling her office when she was hit by a stone in her face. Even before she could realize what was happening, three to four men advanced towards her, pelting stones. In the lead were Philips and Suresh Bhaskar, another trusted Gawli aide. Ramaswamy managed to escape with injuries to her face and made her way to her office, after which she was taken to the Hinduja Hospital. She also filed a complaint with the Agripada police, and while Bhaskar was arrested the same day, Philips was picked up a day later.

Needless to say, as soon as he secured bail, Philips was back in his little office in the Dagdi Chawl, spewing even more hatred against the police.

The Gawli gang stuck to its claim of being the victim and not the villain till the very end. In fact, soon after, Philips and thirteen others were arrested again for Bukhari's murder and a large amount of arms and ammunition were seized from them. Gawli's wife called a press conference at the Mumbai Marathi Patrakar Sangh hall in south Mumbai, at which she claimed that she knew of a plot where Dawood had paid off the Mumbai police to murder her husband.

Philips' Journey to Priesthood

Philips left the gang in the early 2000s, after the gang's influence started to peter out. He went to his native place with his wife, where he quickly got involved with the local church. Soon, he became a priest himself.

Old-timers in the gang still chuckle at his transformation. '*Aapla Philips aata Father jhala aahe*,' they say in amused wonder, referring to his priesthood by the colloquial name for padre.

Not much is known about the circumstances surrounding Philips' exit from the gang. There are some who say he had turned informer in the later years, a claim that is scoffed at by many, given his loyalty to Gawli. However, multiple sources have claimed to have seen him visiting senior police officers on more than one occasion.

This was also the time when some of Gawli's loyal members started turning on him. The worst impact of this was observed when Shrikrishna Gaurav helped police with vital information about the murder of Shiv Sena corporator Kamalakar Jamsandekar in 2007. Another aide, Sandeep Gangan, turned approver in the case, and Gawli was convicted for the murder.

Whether or not Philips crossed over to the other side, in 2005 he submitted a written application to the Mumbai police claiming that he feared for his life as Gawli was trying to have him killed, a claim that was rubbished by Gawli.

Philips' last brush with fame was in 2006, and for a very unusual reason, considering his repertoire of murder, assault and extortion cases. When Indian astronaut Sunita Williams went on her first space expedition, he held a prayer meeting for her safe return. Concern for her well-being was very high among Indians, as Kalpana Chawla, another Indo-American astronaut, had lost her life in the Space Shuttle Columbia disaster in 2003.

The *Indian Express* carried an interview with him, in which he was quoted as saying he was doing God's work. The article made it to the front page anchor and was later followed up by television channels.

Raju Philips' transformation from Gawli's work to God's work was astonishing.

Last heard, Raju had hit the road in a mission to conduct prayer meetings and to spread the message of Jesus, the Messiah.

The execution of Bukhari through the Gawli gang instead of Dawood men was the Maharashtra minister's masterstroke. He killed two birds in one stroke. He had got Bukhari killed and eliminated a major threat to his political career which was already in the doldrums. And after it was found that the Gawli gang was behind the killing, it could only be surmised that perhaps Bukhari was killed for communal reasons or his association with the Dawood gang. The killing could never be connected to the minister or to his threat of exposing him.

Police sources said the politician could have asked Dawood to bump off Bukhari, but the subsequent arrests would have only established the minister's nexus with Dawood, which was at the heart of the conflict between him and Bukhari.

HITMAN 9

Bulletproof Bora Becomes Baba

An Unlikely Yogi

He walks with a limp, is short and wiry and would not elicit a second glance if he walked down a crowded street in any area apart from Dharavi and Chembur, where everyone knows who he is. They know that the strength of the nondescript man lies in the sheer clout that he seems to wield, and they are aware of the awe-inspiring incidents he has committed that have contributed into shaping the legend of the man. Until his arrest, he was known as the Yogi Baba of Sion, while the police called him 'DK of Dharavi'.

His given name is Ravi Mallesh Bora, a name that not many would remember today. Say the name D. K. Rao, however, and anyone's eyes would light up in recognition, along with no small measure of respect, however grudging.

Rao came to Mumbai from his native Gulbarga in Karnataka with his parents, who migrated to the metropolis to escape the persecution that their tribe, the Barias, had been suffering right from the time of the British Raj. The denotified tribe was among the many declared as criminal tribes by the erstwhile rulers of the country, leading to years and years of indignity and hard labour. Rao's father brought his family to Mumbai to try and give them a better life. Little did he know that, fifty years later, his son's name would overshadow every other name in his family tree.

While Rao's father devoted himself to trying to earn an honest buck by working in the Prakash Cotton Mills in Lower Parel, a young Ravi, who had a job as a watchman at a residential building in Dharavi, was least interested in hard work and an honest livelihood. In his free time, Ravi roamed around the Matunga-Wadala area, striking up friendships with other youth with a similar bent of mind: the desire to make a fast buck with as little effort as possible. He was but a teenager when he got involved in a street fight outside Khalsa College, thus earning his first FIR and a history with the Mumbai police records. But Ravi was destined for bigger things than roadside brawls.

It was in 1996 that a twenty-year-old Ravi, along with the rag-tag group of young men he had brought together, committed his first organized crime. The targets of choice for robberies in those days were vans leaving from banks after loading up the cash from their vaults, to be taken to lockers for safe storage. Rao's fledgling gang struck one such van after days of reconnaissance and planning, making away with nothing less than Rs 2.5 million in cash, a fortune most could only dream of back in the 1990s.

The success of their first job gave Ravi's gang a boost of confidence, and the young man went on to execute a string of robberies along with various friends, one of them being Ramnarayan Gupta, alias Lakhan Bhaiya, another name as well known as D. K. Rao in the annals of the underworld.

Lakhan Bhaiya was shot dead in an encounter in Andheri in 2006 by a team led by encounter specialist Pradeep Sharma and his hit squad. Lakhan and his friend Anil Bheda were picked up from Vashi by Sharma, and while Bheda was later released, Lakhan was found dead near the Nana Nani Park in Versova. Lakhan's brother, Ramprasad Gupta, went to court and accused Sharma's team of having staged the encounter.

A special investigation team, headed by then deputy commissioner of police K. M. M. Prasanna, was formed to investigate the case, and after a long court-monitored inquiry, the SIT arrested Sharma in 2010. He was then sent to judicial custody while the trial began. The trial was as dramatic as the encounter, with Anil Bheda, the star witness in the case, going missing in the middle of the trial. Bheda's partially-burned dead body was later found in Yeoor Hills in Thane district, and in 2013, Sharma was acquitted by the court.

The same Lakhan Bhiaya who is credited with driving the last nail in the coffin of Sharma's career as a policeman is also believed to have been instrumental in giving D. K. Rao to the Chhota Rajan gang.

By the second half of 1996, Ravi had a string of cases to his name in police stations all over the city. It was as if no cash van was safe from him and his gang of robbers—they struck hard, struck fast and fled faster. It did not take long for the Mumbai police to start taking in interest in this young man who seemed to be the talk of the town, and soon informants were being leaned on for any and every scrap of information that could be gleaned about his movements and whereabouts. With that kind of pressure, something has to give. Something or the other did, and in late 1996, Ravi found himself under arrest.

He was then sent to the Thane central jail where his association with Lakhan Bhaiya, along with his reputation as a master robber, *choron ka raja*, earned him an entry into the Rajan camp.

At the time, the Rajan coterie in the Thane jail was led by Sunil Madgaonkar, alias Matya bhai, an enforcer and recruiter for Rajan, who had by this time parted ways with Dawood. Matya was arrested in 1997 while he was trying to cross over to Nepal. The then police commissioner Subhash Malhotra described him as the CEO of the Chhota Rajan gang. Matya was so powerful and influential that, during lunch hour at a court hearing in Esplanade Court in Azaad Maidan, he had spread out a massive seven-course feast for all his men present in the court.

Hussain Zaidi and I had met Matya and interviewed him while he was devouring his meal hungrily. He answered Hussain's questions between wolfing down huge morsels of tandoori chicken and biryani. Hussain later reproduced that interview in the *Indian Express* under the headline 'Chhota Rajan, Badi Baat'. What surprised me at the time was Matya's indifference towards the police escort team, his mega feast for his men and his willingness to share intricate details of the gang with us.

The Chief of Thieves

Ostensibly outraged over Dawood's participation in the 1993 bomb blasts, Rajan had by this time started trying hard to project himself as a 'Hindu don' and vowed to exact revenge for Dawood's *'deshdroh'*, treason. To be able to match the strength of the D-Company, Rajan was going to need lot of men, and was hence forever on the lookout for newer talent. The young Ravi, who Matya bhai inducted into his gang, proved to be an asset beyond Matya bhai's or even Rajan's wildest expectations.

Once out of prison, Ravi resumed his spree of robberies and dacoities, but this time for the Rajan gang. It was also around this time that he assumed the name that would become his identity for the rest of his life. It is surmised that, one day, he found an ID card among his things in the name of a bank employee—D. K. Rao. Perhaps it was something he had brought home along with the loot from one of the many cash vans he swooped down on. He decided to carry the card with him so that he could use it in a common trick employed by history-sheeters to hide their identity in case they were caught committing a crime. Ravi Mallesh Bora already had a long record to his name by now, and if he was stopped in a random check in any part of the city, he would automatically be taken aside for questioning. D. K. Rao, on the other hand, was a nobody and would not elicit much suspicion in such a situation, unless someone remembered and recognized his face. Hence, Ravi started carrying the card with him.

The trick, however, not only failed to work but led to the legend of D. K. Rao. In 1997, Sub-Inspector Mridula Lad, who was with the Juhu police station, received a tip-off that Ravi, along with an accomplice, was going to commit a dacoity in her jurisdiction, and reached the spot specified by her informant. When Ravi and his friend reached the area, they found the police team waiting for them. Lad accosted the duo and asked them to surrender, but they shot at her, missing her by inches. Lad shot back and hit Rao in the leg. He fell to the ground while his accomplice managed to escape in the ensuing confusion.

Following the skirmish, both of them, criminal and cop, were catapulted to fame for different reasons.

Lad became the first lady encounter cop and inspired many young women to shoot if necessary and kill if you must. Many gutsy women followed in her footsteps, killing several criminals in encounters, at times stealing the limelight from their male counterparts.

While Ravi was rushed to the hospital for treatment, the police, based on the ID card found in his pocket, registered a case against him identifying him as D. K. Rao. It was only much later that the cops learned that D. K. Rao and Ravi Mallesh Bora were the same person. The name, however, stuck, and when Rao hobbled out of jail, now with a permanent limp thanks to the bullet he had taken in his leg, he was addressed as either 'DK' or 'Rao' by his fellow gang members.

The next time that the police came face-to-face with D. K. Rao would be an occasion that no one would ever forget. The day was 11 November 1998. The climate in Mumbai was best described as blood-soaked, with the war between Dawood and Rajan at its peak. Rajan, as part of his 'patriotic' vendetta against Dawood, had taken to killing D-gang members who were part of the 1993 bomb blasts, and Rao, who had already gained Rajan's trust by this time, was tasked with these missions. After adding several scalps to his belt, Rao was on that day on his way to kill two more men. One of them was Shaikh Mohammed Ehtesham, charged with being part of the team that received the arms and ammunition in Raigad, while the other, Baba Moosa Chauhan, was charged with delivering AK-56 automatic rifles to the residence of actor Sanjay Dutt. Both had been convicted and were sentenced to ten years of rigourous imprisonment, and, having challenged the conviction in a higher court, were on their way to attend a hearing, which was when Rao planned to strike.

Unknown to Rao and his team, another man as feared as himself was on his way to intercept him: senior inspector with the Mumbai police Crime Branch, Ambadas Pote, known for his fiercely loyal approach to his job and daring encounters. Now retired, Pote remains one of the go-to persons for all things underworld and can recall any story about the Dawood or Rajan gangs at the mere mention of a keyword.

Dramatic Dance of Death at Dadar

Having learned about Rao's plan, Pote was on that day speeding to stop the gangster before he shed any more blood in the city. The face-off occurred on Sayani Road near Khed Gully: the Maruti Gypsy carrying Pote and his team came face-to-face with the Maruti Esteem bearing Rao and his hit squad. A deadly exchange of fire ensued that sent everyone running helter skelter, ducking for cover and screaming for their lives. The Esteem was pierced by scores of bullets and, in a matter of minutes, its insides were stained with blood.

Guns trained, Pote and his team advanced on the Esteem even as it sunk down on its punctured tyres. The police team pulled open its doors and began dragging out the occupants. The first ones were Raja Gore and Vipin Khanderao, who were dead. Next came Ramesh Pujari, Jairam Shetty and Rao himself, who, unknown to the cops, were semi-conscious but alive. All the five men were dumped into the back of a police van that had reached the spot.

As the van started, Shetty cried out in pain, 'Amma!' Without a word, the policemen turned around and fired several more rounds at the mass of bodies slumped in the back. Shetty and Pujari jerked with the impact of the rounds hitting their bodies and died on the spot, but Rao, who was hidden under both of them, escaped the second volley of bullets.

The van reached KEM Hospital in Parel and drove around to the back where the morgue was. As per procedure, the policemen were taking what they believed to be five dead bodies for postmortem so that the reports could be attached to the inevitable paperwork that followed such encounters. To their utter shock—some of the policemen actually thought they were seeing a ghost—Rao crawled out from under his friends' bodies, bleeding from several bullet wounds and screaming that he was alive. *'Mee jivant aahe, Doctor mala vachwa, help help.'*

The police squad was too stunned to react for the first few seconds. Then all hell broke loose. Other civilians at the morgue started running away in fear, the medical attendants who had come forward to take charge of the bodies stood in confused silence and the policemen went for their guns.

Shouting abuses and threats at the top of their voices, they made Rao come out of the van with his hands raised, after which they turned him over to the doctors. Any thought of shooting him down inside the van itself was quickly discarded for a simple reason: there were too many eye-witnesses.

The desperate pleas of a bleeding, supposedly dying man moved the team of medical professionals present in the ward. They galvanized into action to save the man. The doctors and paramedics presumed that the police team that had carted him there considered his life as precious.

Doctors who operated on Rao would later tell the police that he had been hit by no less than nineteen bullets and had still lived to tell the tale. The next few months led to the spawning of a lot of speculation as to how Rao had survived the assault. Some said that he was able to hold his breath and play dead as he knew yoga. Others said that he used the dead bodies of his friends to shield himself. Yet others said he was just plain lucky. But from that day onwards, his miraculous escape from the jaws of death became the only thing that people would talk about every time his name was mentioned for a long time.

Over the next ten years, Rao had limited contact with the outside world. He first spent around six months in the hospital recovering from his wounds, and then the rest of the ten years in central jails across the state. However, even though he was largely inactive, factors beyond his control conspired to further push him towards his destiny.

The first was Matya bhai's death. Matya was among Rajan's top aides at the time, and one of the most sought-after men towards the late 1990s. While Rajan was holed up in Malaysia, Matya bhai—as he was known in the gang—ran the show in Mumbai. Any gangster who is not based out of India but still wants to have a grip in the country needs a man he can trust on the ground. Someone to recruit and manage footsoldiers, take care of money matters, sanction jobs and provide weaponry and any other equipment needed. Matya bhai was that person for Rajan in India. He was recruited by Rajan back when the latter was still with the D-gang, and was among those who moved out of the gang when Rajan severed ties with Dawood. Matya bhai's kills included the head of East West airlines Thakiyuddin Wahid, businessman Mahesh Dholakia and Arun Gawli's shooter Ashok Joshi.

While these kills earned him a place of fear in the minds of the people and respect in the eyes of the underworld, it also earned him the ire of the police who, by this time, had started either gunning down Rajan's men in encounters or locking them up for long spells under the Maharashtra Control of Organised Crime Act. So stringent is the act that it denies even the chance of bail for around a year after an accused is arrested. Policemen still fall over themselves trying to meet all the criteria to apply MCOCA against particularly irksome history-sheeters so that they can be put away for a couple of years.

Ringleader Rao

As part of this cleanup operation, Matya bhai was killed in a police encounter in 2000. Suddenly Rajan found himself without a trustworthy aide in India. Still, D. K. Rao was the last name on his mind in terms of a replacement. Sure, Rao was good, but not good enough for Rajan to hand over Matya bhai's throne to him. Rao was just one of the many aides that Rajan had in his syndicate. His loyalists included O. P. Singh, Bharat Nepali, Ejaz Lakdawala, Rohit Verma, Balu Dokre, Fareed Tanasha, Santosh Shetty and Vicky Malhotra, and they ran the gang's affairs.

Then came the second twist of fate. In the same year,

Rajan was attacked by a group of assassins sent by Dawood's right-hand man Shakeel Babumiyan Sheikh, alias Chhota Shakeel. It was Shakeel's lifelong dream to please his boss by killing the traitor who not only turned his back on the gang but had gone on to project himself as a patriot, thereby taking all the sympathy and painting Dawood as the villain. This dream almost came to fruition on 15 September 2000, when Munna Jhingada led a hit squad that barged into an apartment in Bangkok where Rajan was partying. The killers first pumped Rajan's trusted aide Rohit Verma full of bullets and then proceeded to shoot at Rajan, who managed to escape.

The attack lead to the near decimation of the Rajan gang, with some of the key members breaking away and others being killed over the next few years. One of them, O. P. Singh, was killed in Nashik jail by none other than Rao himself in 2002.

Singh had joined Rajan's gang after his brother, Arun Singh, was killed by the Ashwin Naik gang. Unlike most members of the gang, who were barely educated and had turned to crime to earn money and respect the easy way, Singh was a chemistry postgraduate employed as a Quality Control Officer at the Mazgaon docks. After his brother was murdered, he named the Naik gang in his police complaint, causing the gang to target him. Singh knew some Rajan gang members after coming into contact with them in a bar in Chembur; he sought their help, and was thus inducted into the gang.

Like many other foot soldiers, he started off

committing robberies and dacoities, and soon moved on to kidnappings and murders. What set him apart was his analytical mind, thanks to his education, and he soon started advising Rajan in several matters. He also built contacts for Rajan in police and political circles in India, particularly in Mumbai, which earned him a place in Rajan's inner circle in Kuala Lumpur, where he added several more feathers to his cap, including the murder of Mirza Dilshad Beg, a Nepali minister and a high-ranking Dawood Ibrahim aide, in Kathmandu in 1998. He even assumed charge of the gang after the attempt on Rajan's life and coordinated with lawyers and the Thai media while his boss recuperated in hospital. In November 2000, when Rajan escaped from the Smitivej Hospital in Bangkok, Singh was the one who got the credit for orchestrating it.

There are still multiple theories about why Singh was killed. One theory is that some members of Rajan's gang were jealous of his growing popularity and poisoned their boss' ears against him. Ironically, this is exactly what had happened to Rajan. Shakeel and a few others, irked by Rajan's closeness to Dawood, started feeding stories against Rajan to Dawood. These stories reached Rajan's ears and he fled from a party in Dubai where he suspected he was going to be killed, and ran straight into the arms of Indian intelligence agencies.

When Rajan became suspicious of Singh, having heard Balu Dokre's stories about him wanting to break away and form his own gang, Rajan tipped off Indian law enforcement agencies about his movements. When

Singh landed at New Delhi airport in 2002, a team of policemen was waiting for him. He was handed over to the Mumbai police, who brought him to the city and placed him under arrest. He was then sent to Nashik jail while investigations against him progressed. Knowing that Rajan hated him, he thought he was safe inside a central jail. What he didn't count on was D. K. Rao.

Pulling heaven knows what strings, Rao, who was in Arthur Road central jail after his return from the dead, got himself transferred to the Nashik jail. The murder, which went down in police files as one of the most brutal ones ever recorded, took place on a Sunday afternoon. Singh was playing cricket with some other inmates, and in the middle of the match, he felt a tap on his shoulder. He turned to see a fellow inmate standing behind him.

'OP, *zara side mein aa na*,' the man said, asking Singh to come aside. He led Singh to a corner of the prison yard, where Rao, along with thirteen others, was waiting for him. Before Singh could realize what was happening, the group pounced on him, raining blows and kicks on him from all sides till he could barely move.

When Singh, who himself was tall and solidly built, had stopped thrashing about, the group parted and Rao coolly walked forward. Wordlessly, he walked around a cowering Singh, knelt down and cradled Singh's head in his hands and slipped a jute rope around it. A severely-beaten but still conscious Singh clawed at the rope around his neck and the hands holding them but Rao held fast, staring expressionlessly into his prey's terrified eyes till he had stopped struggling. Rao's henchmen watched in horrified awe as he drained the life out of Singh, straightened up casually, turned around and walked away. After another few seconds of staring fascinatedly at the dead man before them, the others walked away too.

A subsequent inquiry by the prisons department revealed that Rao had bribed several prisons officials so that he could get thirteen members of the Rajan gang transferred to Nashik jail to help him with the murder. Rao had clearly taken into account Singh's physical prowess and made sure he had enough manpower to overpower and subdue his target.

Among the other remaining members of Rajan's inner circle, Ejaz Lakdawala, Santosh Shetty and Ravi Pujari left to form their own gangs. Shetty was deported from Bangkok in 2011 after lengthy efforts by the Mumbai Crime Branch, and brought to Mumbai to stand trial for his crimes. Lakdawala and Pujari have managed to evade the law and somehow keep their shops open, although both have been facing the same problem: the lack of loyal footsoldiers.

For Pujari, the problem is that he does not take care of his men once they are arrested, which makes them lose faith. Although there is no absence of poor, uneducated men willing to turn to crime for a fast buck, word travels fast in the underworld when you don't care about your men. In fact, inmates of central jails who have worked for Ravi Pujari and have been abandoned by him are known as members of the 'condom' gang, as they are used and thrown by Pujari.

Lakdawala, meanwhile, is suffering from an absence of effective recruiters. He opened another can of worms for the prisons department in November 2016, when the Mumbai Crime Branch arrested three of his shooters for plotting to kill a Jogeshwari-based businessman who refused to pay him extortion money. It was revealed that the orders had come from Lakdawala through his aide Prashant Rao, who is in Nashik central jail. The prisons department has initiated an inquiry to find out how Prashant Rao, who is relatively small fry in the underworld, managed to get a cell phone and run the gang's affairs from inside the jail.

Thus, both Pujari and Lakdawala are managing to keep their heads above the water with whatever money they get from whoever they manage to scare enough into paying up. Balu Dokre was murdered by Shakeel's men in Malaysia in 2005, while Bharat Nepali, who had left with Santosh Shetty, was killed in Bangkok in 2011. Farid Tanasha was shot dead in his own house in Mumbai in 2010. Vicky Malhotra, one of Rajan's closest aides, is managing Rajan's affairs in the northeast, while those that helped with Singh's murder, including Sarfira Nepali and Bala Parab, were killed in police encounters in the days to come.

And so it was that, due to a combination of factors, Rao remained the only old-time Rajan gang member to survive and was by default elevated to a senior post in the gang, doing for Rajan what Rajan once did for Dawood Ibrahim Kaskar.

It is said that Rao still recruits petty criminals into

the Rajan fold, and eventually gives them bigger jobs, like murders, to handle. He is also known to be a good manager, always taking care of his men. Whenever any of his men are arrested, he arranges for money and sureties for their bail, and takes care of their families while they are behind bars, automatically earning a place of respect and trust in the minds of his men.

After Singh's murder, Rao spent seven more years in prison before being released on bail. Always the favourite child of the limelight it did not take long for him to be in the news again.

Jail, Bail, Jail

The controversy this time was not actually around D. K. Rao but the people who attended the lavish party that was thrown to celebrate his release from jail. His men lost no time in organizing a Christmas bash in his honour in December 2009, and around a week after the party, an English daily reported that the party was attended by at least six personnel from the Mumbai police, including an assistant commissioner of police. A short video clip of the cops dancing along with Rao's men went viral on social media shortly thereafter. The cops were suspended immediately and a departmental inquiry was initiated into the matter. The incident, however, proved that Rao had not lost his touch for expanding his clout and making contacts within the police force.

Around this time, the author Joseph Campana requested Hussain Zaidi to interview Rao for his anthology on Dharavi. As usual I tagged along with Joseph and Hussain to meet the top gangster in flesh and blood.

Rao had bought a huge office in the Sion-Dharavi area and set up an organization called Bhrashtachar Virodhi Manch (Anti Corruption Forum). A board at the entrance of the office announced this, along with another board, which indicated that he was a labour organization activist of Mathadi Kamgar Union. The office, which was made after joining two 225-sq feet rooms into one unit, screamed of affluence and prosperity. Rao had recently been released on bail, and yet he was able to operate from such a plush office. There were nine phones, including a couple of satellite phones, on the table in front of Rao, who was himself busy working on a tablet. A lawyer sat by at Rao, and he countered every question put forth by Campana and Hussain about Rao's past and underworld activities with an argument. After this had gone on for a while between the lawyer and us, Rao finally interjected, 'I do property work. People consult me on property matters especially in Sector 4 of Sion, Dharavi and other places of Antop Hill.'

When questioned about his criminal past, Rao said he was a reformed man. 'I believe in the doctrine of Nirankari Baba and Swami Samarth and practise yoga as taught to me by Art of Living volunteers. In fact, I also met Sri Sri Ravi Shankar when he came to Borivali.'

After some mundane conversation, he said with an enigmatic smile, 'Now I teach yoga on my building terrace to all the youngsters of the area.' Hussain had heard that the classes included martial arts, and suspected that Rao's smile was because of this.

Rao's lackeys were getting increasingly uncomfortable with our presence. They did not allow the interview to last long.

Once outside they told us that it was time for 'Baba' to rest, and it was inconvenient for him to entertain us anymore.

The whole set-up gave us the sense that he had no intention of retiring, despite him setting up an NGO against corruption, becoming a follower of Sant Nirankari Baba and claiming to be a reformed man. It took only a few months for this theory to be proven right. Rao was arrested for a daring shootout right outside the residence of Dawood Ibrahim Kaskar's brother Iqbal, in which Iqbal's driver lost his life. The three shooters, supposedly on orders from Rao, lay in wait at Pakmodia Street, traditionally known as the epicentre of the Kaskar family's power in Mumbai, and opened fire at Iqbal's driver, Arif Bael (bael means bullock; here it means buffoon), when he came out of the house to start the car for his boss.

It is assumed that the shooters were told to kill Iqbal Kaskar but ended up killing Bael instead. Another theory is that Rao knew that Iqbal would not be so easy to get to, but wanted to send a message to Dawood nonetheless. Killing Iqbal's personal driver sent a message all right, one that travelled all the way to Pakistan and made Dawood seethe with anger. The incident was less of an attack and more of an insult for him. He immediately instructed his man Friday, Chhota Shakeel, to teach the impudent upstart a lesson.

Rao, over the next three years, went on to be charged with several other cases of extortion, and was back in jail. During this time, he was also questioned in connection with the murder of veteran journalist Jyotirmoy Dey. Dey was shot dead in June 2011 a short while after he left his residence in Powai on his bike. Subsequent investigations revealed that Dey had managed to rub Rajan the wrong way, leading to the don ordering a hit on the investigative journalist. Rao was among the several Rajan aides questioned by the Mumbai Crime Branch in their quest for information about the murder, a logical step due to his prominent position in the gang and his closeness to his boss.

Three years later, in 2014, the Pakmodia Street shootout came back to haunt him. Shakeel finally managed to find out enough about Rao's schedule and planned a hit. Rao, who was in Nashik jail at the time, was being produced in the Sessions Court regularly in connection with the trial in the Pakmodia Street shootout. Shakeel hired two shooters, Mohammed Siddiqui and Akhtar Khan, to kill Rao as well as Ashok Satardekar, another old-time Rajan aide.

The plan, according to Crime Branch officers, was to bump him off when he was brought to the Sessions Court on 4 September. Luck, however, favoured Rao a third time. A few days after Siddiqui reached Mumbai and started staying with Khan, awaiting further orders, the Anti Extortion Cell of the Mumbai Crime Branch got a tip-off that something big was going to go down soon. Police Inspector Vinayak Vast, in charge of the AEC, and his subordinate Jaywant Sankpal, leaned on their informants and pulled out all stops to find out what was in the offing, and on 4 September, they arrested Siddiqui and Khan, seizing a .32 bore revolver and four live rounds from them. The duo had been told explicitly to kill Rao first, and then move on to Satardekar. Life, it seems, has a soft corner for D. K. Rao. No amount of bullets appears capable of killing him.

The last indicator of Rao's clout and activity, as well as the fact that prisons in Maharashtra are now second home to him, came in June 2015, when he was lodged in the Taloja central jail. A surprise check of his cell revealed three mobile phones, which were seized by the prisons department. The phones were presented at the MCOCA court where Rao was being tried for a case against him at the time, and the court ordered the Navi Mumbai police to conduct an investigation against him.

The *Hindu*, in the very first issue of its Mumbai edition launched on 28 November, reported that when the Navi Mumbai police obtained call data records of the three cell phones and analyzed them, they found that no less than five hundred calls had been made using the three cell phones over a period of five to six months, and a large chunk of these calls had been to international numbers. The prisons department, meanwhile, conducted an inquiry of its own and found four prisons staff members guilty of helping Rao get the cell phones. All four were suspended for a period of four months, and full-fledged departmental inquiries were initiated against each of them.

The timing of these calls to international numbers is pertinent because Rajan, who is now in the custody of the Central Bureau of Investigation after being arrested in Bali in October 2015, was very much active in foreign countries at the time. Rao is suspected to have been in regular touch with Rajan and several of his aides abroad through these cell phones till the time that his boss was caught and brought to India.

HITMAN 10
The Saga of Sunil and Sulaiman

En route to Dubai

The man gently toyed with the revolver on the table. Drops of whiskey formed little condensed pearls on his favorite gun. He took a sip from the glass and slid the gun into his pocket. The yacht swayed gently on the Persian Gulf as it headed towards Dubai and one man's complete freedom.

'Sulaiman Bhai, boss ka phone hai aapke liye,' a boy in a white shirt said, handing a phone to him.

The man was wide-shouldered, burly, and of medium height—five feet eight inches. He looked fearless. He had a square jaw, a clean-shaven face, and filled-out cheeks. The eyes were a misleading window. A naïve soul would have mistaken him for the average Indian common man—he looked like a well-fed central government employee. Neither his eyes nor his healthy face—usually calm and collected—betrayed his profession. He seldom smiled, but he didn't have a grouchy demeanour. He had a deformity in his left ring finger duly noted and filed away in the tomes of various police stations in Mumbai where he was a wanted man.

The man took the phone from the boy, mumbled a few words, nodded in agreement, and then hung up. He went back to his drinks, pulling the woman sitting next to him closer. He relished the fact that, at that exact moment, as much as he was wanted by the Indian police, he was protected by his beloved boss, Dawood Ibrahim.

Sulaiman was sitting peacefully, watching the sun drift lazily past the clear waters, when the boy in the white shirt took a seat opposite him and told him that Chhota Rajan, who had by then left Dawood's gang, wanted him dead. It was six o'clock in the evening, there wasn't a cloud in the sky, and up until that point, Sulaiman had been in a good mood.

Sunil Sawant aka Sautya

Born Sunil Sawant and nicknamed Sautya, the terror tales of this hitman from the Dawood gang begins from the time he was sixteen and had committed his first murder. He was done being bullied by Bhau Marathe, the brother of a powerful Shiv Sena leader from Girgaum. On a clear day in February 1982, Sautya decided to avenge the insults Marathe had thrown at him. He spotted Marathe sitting near a shop in Girgaum. With the stealth and calmness of a tiger approaching its prey, Sautya walked up to Marathe, who was engaged in a deep conversation with his friend. He tapped Marathe on his shoulder to draw his attention. The moment the unsuspecting Marathe turned, without a words or a warning sign, Sautya dug into his pockets and drew out a chopper. Before a bewildered Marathe could react, Sautya stabbed him like a mad man. A bloodied Marathe fell to the ground. Marathe's friend and the passersby were too stunned to react and Sautya smirked and sauntered away like a man without a care in the world.

Sautya was a native of Kaarewadi in Sindhudurg district of Maharashtra, and his father worked as a railway ticket collector in Mumbai. A government job meant that Sautya had a fairly comfortable upbringing as compared to other boys who lived in Girgaum. His father put him in south-central Mumbai's prestigious Marathi-medium school, Chikitsak Samuha Shirolkar High School. It was an old institution, set up way back in 1906 and its students were known for their academic brilliance and stood first in the state's Secondary School Certificate (SSC) exams. The school has produced some of the state's finest writers, poets, scientists, economists, professors and doctors. The teachers at the institution were very inspiring too. So it was a surprise when Sautya simply dropped out of school before completing his tenth standard.

For him were not the laurels of academia. Since the age of fourteen, Sunil Sawant had been emboldened by his own bravura and recklessness. He had formed his own gang while in the Chikitsak School, much to the horror of the staff. His boy gang had three members: Santosh Lad, Manoj Kulkarni and Bachi Apte. Like Sunil, the other three boys were also well-built and sturdy and they infused terror with their mere appearance.

Now, the world beyond Chikitsak beckoned, and this precocious boy plunged into it with much ado. At the age of sixteen, he crossed over to the abyss, knowing fully well that it was a one-way ticket. Bhau Marathe was no small fish in the pond. His brother was in the Shiv Sena, already very popular in the '70s as it was advocating rights for sons-of-the-soil. The Shiv Sena supremo, Bal Thackeray, was the uncanonised godfather of Maharashtra and his pull with Marathi-speaking Maharashtrians was tremendous. Killing a Shiv Sainik in Girgaum was Sautya's Valkyrie moment.

But the throne for the ultimate gang supremacy in the area had come with a battle. Dashrat Rahane was another gangster rising to glory. Based in Kranti Nagar, Rahane had managed to get something that Sautya couldn't: a friendship with the gangster Amar Naik. Rahane had cast his extortion net around the steel traders and market at V. P. Market, and owed his allegiance to none other than Naik.

Sautya competed with Rahane for a while, hoping that Naik would be drawn towards him and ditch Dashrath. When he failed to make headway with Naik, he thought he would do away with the competition. He didn't know how or when, but Rahane nettled him, and he didn't like nettlesome adversaries.

It was Raksha Bandhan, the festival that binds siblings to one another. Sautya met his married sister, Surekha Parab, to get his rakhi tied around his wrist. Surekha was his older sister and she constantly fretted about his wayward ways. He handed her a handsome amount as a return gift for the rakhi. She had prepared a sumptuous lunch for him on the occasion. He had just finished his lunch when he was interrupted by a message from his close aide, Avadhoot Bonde. Surekha wondered what had come over her brother—he suddenly seemed all charged and ready to go. He didn't even wait to say the customary goodbyes.

Bonde had called to say that he tracked down Rahane; he was last seen in a bar near Lalbaugh, enjoying a drink with his friend Surendra Nair.

Sautya asked Bonde to wait for him near Ganesh Talkies at Lalbaugh. He took a cab from Bhootachiwadi in Girgaum and reached Lalbaugh around half past three. It was hardly a fifteen-minute ride. Bonde greeted him with a welcoming hug. The men then took their positions outside the bar. Sautya warned Bonde that Rahane was to die only by his hands. Bonde could keep Nair for himself. An hour later, Rahane and his friend Nair both stepped out, sozzled to their gills. But despite his inebriated state, he spotted Sautya and Bonde. Sautya looked at Rahane and smirked. An uncontrolled round of gunshots followed. Rahane and Nair both dropped to the ground, dead.

And so, by the age of twenty-four, Sautya, having notched two high-profile murders under his belt, got the attention of none other than the Big D, Dawood Ibrahim himself. Dawood was always scouting for men like Sautya. Good breeding but wrong wiring. Men who had been consumed by and convinced of their invincibility.

Men who were fired up from within. Men who did not hesitate to snuff out lives; who did not blink when their quarry collapsed in a helpless mass. Men who were anti-heroes. Men whose hearts were black as coal dust, men whose souls were mortgaged to the devil himself.

After Dashrath Rahane was dispatched to the dungeons of hell, Sautya finally won over Amar Naik. He filled Rahane's shoes easily. They were big ones to fill, considering that Rahane had entrenched himself as Naik's pointman. But it took no time for Sautya to fill the hearts of traders with dread at the mere sound of his footsteps. Meanwhile, Sautya ignored Dawood Ibrahim's overtures. It was a practical choice as, having bumped off Rahane to gain the attention of Amar Naik, he didn't want to upset Naik by switching loyalties. But Dawood did not like being rebuffed and so he did what he does best—played Machiavellian.

Dawood kept a track of Sautya's movements and then tipped off the police, who caught Sautya red-handed with extortion money. After his arrest, Dawood sent Sharad Shetty, alias Anna, who was a Dawood acolyte and also Sautya's friend, to bail him out. Sautya was overwhelmed by Sharad Shetty's kindness, not knowing that he had perfectly landed in the net that Dawood had pitched for him. And so Dawood won over the dauntless youth from Girgaum and Sautya jumped ships from the Amar Naik gang to the D-gang.

After the initial welcome-aboard party, Dawood wasted no time in testing Sautya. He was tasked with two eliminations. Both men, Chennu and Pappu, were from Dawood's bête noire, the Pathan gang. Sautya wanted to prove his worth so he enhanced his challenge by stacking another plate on the barbell. He told Dawood that he would liquidate Chennu and Pappu on their own turf—in Nagpada in central Mumbai.

For the job, he was paired with another new recruit, Anil Parab, a wasted youth reeling from a lot of complexities both in the mind and body.

Sautya and Parab set off on a bike. The Pathan duo was usually seen in the busy market areas of Nagpada, and therefore easy to find. Parab skidded to a stop right in front of their stunned faces and, in a quick motion, Sautya pulled out his revolver and shot at the men. He dispatched quick rounds of bullets into their bodies, killing both Chennu and Pappu on the spot.

Sautya was on cloud nine. He had proved his mettle in the new gang. He was now the D-Company's favourite hitman.

The Dholakia Brothers

In 1987 and 1988, the mafia wars in Mumbai played out like a Western movie. The transition from the older era to the younger era of dons was marked by violence, bloodshed, and murders of rival gang members in broad daylight. The tumult in Afghanistan and Sri Lanka was a boon for the mafia as they upgraded their Colts for lethal AK-47s.

Dawood Ibrahim was, of course, the master puppeteer, and he was slowly eliminating other players.

Among the big players dabbling in both the mafia and supposedly legitimate businesses were the Dholakia brothers—Arvind Dholakia and Mahesh Dholakia.

Arvind had been small fry in the Sopariwala gang and was first arrested on the charge of smuggling in 1974. He was released along with Haji Mastan and Yusuf Patel under an amnesty scheme for smugglers. In the '80s, the brothers grabbed a lot of eyeballs after they emerged as the frontrunners in the real estate business. A couple of restaurants and hotels (Slip Disc, Caesar's Palace, Fisherman's Wharf) that had gained notoriety as organized prostitution joints further cemented the reputation of the brothers. After Sonia Mahal, Caesar's Palace was the precursor to the beer bar dancing hotels in Mumbai. The brothers were arrested again in 1985 under the National Security Act (NSA), but released after two months. Arvind Dholakia had been in and out of the city police records since 1979 with seven cases of rioting and murder filed against him.

The rise to power and glory is often a steep climb and the Dholakia brothers were in danger of tripping when they chose to cross paths with Dawood Ibrahim. Dawood did not like the Dholakia brothers. And neither did other gangsters like Bada Rajan. Arvind and Mahesh were emerging as a powerful force in the lucrative real estate scene and the flesh-trade. For the mafia, this was exactly in conflict with their interests. The mafia didn't like the Dholakias eating into their market share. When the brothers began to feel the heat, they lost no time in aligning themselves with the mafia, including Arun

Gawli, to fund their activities. Unlike other businessmen, the Dholakias were not just funding the mafia, they were actively part of the mafia. Dawood decided to eliminate them before they became too big for their boots.

For Dawood and Chhota Rajan, Sautya was the go-to man to finish Mahesh Dholakia. In April 1987, Mahesh Dholakia emerged in a Maruti car from his Pedder Road residence and immediately noticed the tail. Six men were crammed in the car and their malevolence was manifest even without a single threatening gesture. He immediately took a left turn, abandoned his car, and ran into a building, fear writ large on his face. Death was knocking at the door and his legs were trembling. His hands were clammy and his heart was pounding so loud, he thought even his killers could hear the deafening thud. His eyes were big orbs of fear. The killers followed him in. They were not running. They walked behind him and shot him in the leg and, as he lay bleeding, terror-struck, in front of a private garage, Sautya came very close to him and, at point-blank range, silenced the thudding heart and head.

Arvind Dholakia swore revenge on the funeral pyre of his brother. He egged the police on for action against Dawood by constantly squealing about his activities. He even sponsored Arun Gawli for a while, but it is said that it was Gawli—for extortion reasons—who was behind Arvind Dholakia's death in his own cabin at Caesar's Palace, one year after the younger brother was killed.

You cannot play cat and mouse with Dawood and expect to emerge unscathed. The Dholakia brothers came in a whiff and went off in a puff.

Scourge for Gawli

In the fall of 1988, the underworld struck out at each other like mad men on a chess board. Only the best would live to see the rising sun again. This war was ignited not by the constant bloodied rage of gang culture, but by an incident that changed the course of history for the top two gangs of Mumbai. The Mumbai police were at their wits' end but also happy that the gangs were at each other's throats—the hope was that each would decimate the other and make their job much easier.

Satish Raje, a close aide of Dawood who also looked after his accounts and properties in India, was gunned down by Gawli's aide Ashok Joshi. Dawood retaliated by asking Sautya to kill Joshi. Sautya gunned down Joshi near Panvel. Over the next few weeks, both ganglords continued hitting out at each other's close aides. By now, Sautya had killed many men. And, he said, if he had to, he'd do it all over again. After every killing, Sautya slept like a baby—there was a surprising amount of physical exertion in murder. Sautya had turned killing into his passion, becoming more ruthless and bloodthirsty with every passing day. It was clear that he had now made many more enemies, and also got the police desperate to catch or kill him. Dawood realized it was important to take Sautya out of the game for a while and introduce a new face when he was gone. That was the entry point for Subhash Singh Thakur, alias ST, into the underworld.

When Sautya returned, he was given the option to choose his own partner in crime. It came as a surprise to everyone when he chose ST.

Thakur hailed from a farmer family from Uttar Pradesh, but was a Mumbai man for all practical purposes. Unlike everyone else in the D-Company, ST had not chosen to be in the mafia until the time he was forced to. For months, ST would be dragged to jail, detained and beaten up under false claims. The police was under tremendous pressure to arrest gangsters and fill jail cells, and when unable to do so, they would pick innocent men like ST and lash at them. ST bore the brunt of this for months, until he decided to become the gangster that he was accused of being. The criminals in jail had turned ST into one himself. ST got in touch with Chhota Rajan, who employed ST as Sautya's aide. Sautya decided to exploit ST's rage against the system to the advantage of the D-Company. The two of them began to work very closely and acquired an unbeatable reputation as a team.

In the early '90s, Sautya and ST were as savage as they were fearless. Word reached Sautya that Arun Gawli was plotting to kill him and Chhota Rajan. In an act of utter defiance and mockery of the don, Sautya and ST went to Dagdi Chawl, otherwise known as Gawli's headquarters, and opened fire at the gates of the chawl. It was an open challenge posed to Arun Gawli. Chhota Rajan had by then already escaped to Dubai, and Sautya left for Nepal shortly after. Once settled in Kathmandu, Sautya then called for ST to join him. Sautya was the first D-gang member to set up base in Nepal, which not only turned into a hideout point for him, but also an important business centre.

U-Turn for U-Nita

Like every great story of every great warrior, the lady love either wins him the battle, or drives him to his death. With Sautya, the tale took a slow and dramatic turn towards the inevitable fall.

With his growing fame as a feared gangster, women and wine had slowly become Sautya's weaknesses. ST did not approve of this but stood by as a helpless spectator to it all anyway. Sautya had fallen in love. And the lady in question was his best friend Pappi Shirshekar's wife, Unita. She had come to Sautya seeking help for her imprisoned husband. ST warned Sautya against setting his eyes on a married woman, let alone his best friend's wife. This was the first breaking point in the relationship. ST was old-school, old-world values. He was into crime but he was also religious and drew the moral line on many vices.

But Sautya was smitten with Unita. He was determined to win her at any cost. Soon their distress meetings turned into furtive love encounters. The couple was so madly engrossed in each other that they didn't mind eliminating any hurdle that stood in their way. Including Unita's husband and Sautya's best friend.

Sautya arranged for Shirshekar to be released from jail only to have him killed. Witnesses were bought and top lawyers were hired. Soon Shirshekar was released from jail. It became difficult for Sautya and Unita to meet around Shirshekar, so Sautya arranged to have him murdered immediately. Sautya started taking

Shirshekar out for drinks and was publically spotted with him. The duo looked like two old friends who were inseparable. One day, Sautya sent two of his friends to invite Shirshekar for drinks. At the bar, an unidentified man approached the three men and emptied a round of bullets in Shirshekar's chest. Nobody suspected Sautya and the blame was placed on the Gawli gang.

Sautya then offered help and support to Shirshekar's widow Unita, who happily accepted it. From a helpless widow to a gangster's lover, Unita transformed overnight. She began travelling to Kathmandu with Sautya and enjoyed the callous killings that he carried out. The other gang members, especially ST, despised Unita but kept their contempt to themselves. Sautya's undivided attention to Unita distanced him from his gang members. Sautya had begun to break his own rules and let Unita call the shots. ST tried to reason with Sautya, but in vain. This irked ST, who then began to distance himself from Sautya. Their friendship lay on the line for months, until it finally faded away. Their famous alliance was headed for a clear split.

Sautya and Unita got married shortly after. Sautya would always ask Unita to join him whenever he was out on a mission. He used her as a cover to evade cops who had set up *nakabandi* on the drive from Juhu to Pydhonie in south Mumbai. He would drive with Unita as the police generally don't stop couples in private cars.

But a few years later, Sautya lost interest in Unita and began moving around with other women. He also fell in love with a lady named Raziya and eventually married her too. If the police forces are to be believed, in the years to come it would be Sautya's scorned wife Unita who would help Rajan kill Sautya.

Meanwhile, while Sautya was busy romancing women, ST channelized his energy and efforts into becoming the best shooter that the D-Company ever had. His killing instincts became so sharp, that he managed to catch the attention of none other than the don himself, Dawood Ibrahim. ST became one of the very few gang members who were invited to Dawood's house in Dubai to meet him personally. Following which, ST began taking direct orders from Dawood. This did not go down well with any gang member, especially Sautya and Rajan. ST was turning into an asset for the D-Company. He was very focused. He was loyal. He didn't get swayed by women. He didn't wallow in the violence. He did his executions with the precision of a surgeon but didn't dwell on them. He was not flamboyant and he didn't throw his weight around. Unlike Sautya, he came from a humble background.

ST resided in a palatial bungalow in Kathmandu with Sautya. It was a safe hideout for most of Dawood's men. At this time, Chhota Rajan, formerly Dawood's favourite, had begun to feel his position in the D-Company was being threatened. Dawood seemed to be giving more preference and importance to both ST and Sautya, which was making Rajan more bitter by the day.

In what is regarded as one of the most sensational crimes in the history of the underworld, ST and Sautya had killed Shailesh Haldankar and Bipin Shere in the J J shootout in Mumbai in 1992. The duo had executed the public killing to avenge the death of Dawood's brother-in-law, Ibrahim Parker. Following the J J shootout, the police force of the entire country galvanized into action and began hunting Dawood's two most ferocious hitmen. The police had begun to zero-in on any information of the whereabouts of Sautya. They got a lot of leads from none other than Sautya's jilted ex-wife Unita, who squealed about his hideouts and dens. Sautya narrowly escaped being arrested twice but his associates were caught. The police nabbed both Gonde and ST from different hideouts and seized all of their belongings. They also froze all Sautya's financial accounts and raided his properties. For the first time in two decades, it became difficult for Sautya to survive in his own city. After ST's arrest, Sautya was considerably weakened and beginning to get nervous, and nervousness was such an alien emotion to him. The police grip was tighteninng on him and his men, and his hideouts were being raided one after another.

It was around this time that the Crime Branch carried out elaborate raids, desperately trying to finish the D-Company once and for all. In another sensational shootout, the police forces, led by Additional Commissioner Aftab Ahmed Khan, gunned down the infamous Maya Dolas and his three associates in Andheri. Dawood was slowly losing his gems and Sautya had finally begun to fear for his own life.

The shootout at Lokhandwala in which Maya Dolas was killed could have been his own story, Sautya confided to his close aide Manish Lala. Lala looked after the legitimization of Sautya's properties in Mumbai. Once, while travelling in his car from Fort to Powai, Lala narrated the whole story of Sautya to Hussain Zaidi and me in detail.

Sautya wanted to live. With all his men either killed or jailed, Sautya knew he had no choice but to escape. He first absconded to Kathmandu and then headed to Dubai. The turn of events marked a significant change in the history of the underworld. The famous partnership between the killing machines, ST and Sautya had finally come to an end. Sautya neither wanted to get arrested like his crony ST nor did he want to get killed like Maya Dolas. He felt Dubai would be the only safe place for him.

Death Awaited in Dubai

Sautya had converted to Islam in 1995, after arriving in Dubai, and changed his name to Sulaiman. Two decades had passed since he had first washed blood from his hands at the age of sixteen. Countless murders, innumerable affairs and the quintessential life as a hitman of the D-Company had taken its toll. He was now thinking big. He had left India happily for a better and luxurious life in Dubai and closer proximity to his boss Dawood Ibrahim. However, amidst his otherwise smooth move, a dagger of danger was hanging over Sulaiman's head. Chhota Rajan had not forgotten Sautya's political games and the way he had upstaged him and got closer to Dawood. Sautya had also killed his trusted men in Nepal. Rajan had already split with Dawood and his primary targets were Chhota Shakeel and Sautya.

At the same time, Sautya, now Sulaiman, was hatching his own plans of killing Rajan. He became close friends with Chhota Shakeel, who handled the business syndicates of Dawood in Dubai. The two men were preparing for a battle in their own dens and bloodshed was inevitable. Suddenly, the yacht jerked violently and Sulaiman's reverie was broken.

Sulaiman shifted uncomfortably in his seat. He told the boy in the white shirt it was the sea sickness that was making him uncomfortable and asked for his drink to be refilled. Sulaiman also sent the lady away. He knew Rajan would make a move. He just had to make his move before Rajan did. The yacht would dock at the Dubai harbour, and a car would take him straight to Dawood. The idea of being closer to Dawood filled Sulaiman with a sense of calm. He closed his eyes and breathed in the ocean air.

When he reached Dubai, he felt safer from police and his other enemies including Rajan.

For months nothing happened. The two bigwigs of the D-Company lay low and were seemingly occupied with their own business. One day, on 5 August 1995, Sulaiman was out hunting for places to set up his establishment in Deira in Dubai. He told his driver to cut the trip short and head back to the hotel instead. When the car arrived at their hotel, Toofan, Sautya and his Nepalese bodyguard stepped out and headed towards the reception. Just then Sautya heard the loud screech of a car suddenly stop right behind them. He turned around to see four men armed with guns and choppers heading straight towards him. Sautya was unprepared and ambushed.

Without a single word muttered, the men opened fire in Sulaiman's direction. Sulaiman tried to dodge the bullets and stumbled behind his guards. Two bullets had pierced Sulaiman body while he limped for cover. Sautya yelled for his guards to retaliate and fight the assailants. He dragged himself with all his might and began to run away from the men. The men fired more shots. Sulaiman somehow managed to dodge these bullets, limping and running towards the street, screaming in pain and begging for his life. The four men began to chase Sulaiman. In his feeble last attempts to save himself, Sulaiman almost ran into a pole and collapsed to the ground. He tried to cover his profusely bleeding wounds and challenged the men to fight without arms.

His assailants looked at Sulaiman and smirked. The ever-fearless Sulaiman was on the ground pleading to fight for his life. One assailant walked up behind Sulaiman and slashed his throat, while another fired continuous rounds of bullets at his head. Sulaiman breathed his last, falling back into a pool of his own blood.

This gruesome murder was perhaps the first killing carried out on the streets of Dubai by the Mumbai mafia. His assailants left his body on the streets and dialled a number. Sulaiman had been executed. A familiar laugh resounded on the other side of the phone. Rajan had done what nobody could. He had finally put Sulaiman to rest. It also marked the beginning of one of the most lethal gangwars in the history of the mafia—Chhota Rajan had now pitted himself against his former boss, Dawood Ibrahim.

To this day, Chhota Rajan is a wanted man in Dubai. The Dubai police have a look-out notice for him. The assailants from Chhota Rajan's gang were sentenced to death, but not before they pointed fingers at Chhota Rajan.

While it would be easy to dismiss Sautya as just a cog in the wheel of the D-Company, one has to remember that he was the man who executed the big crimes and helped bolster the image of Dawood Ibrahim as the Big Don. Sautya was Dawood's most daring and dangerous hitman. The streak of madness in him made him both an asset and a liability to the organization. But be it businessmen or rival gang members, Sautya never hesitated to take on any killing assignment. From the day he liquidated Bhau Marathe in Girgaum to the time he got killed in Dubai, Sautya was the meanest killing machine that was born on this earth.

HITMAN 11

Dhanda, Danda and Dawood

The Third D

In the Mumbai underworld, there are men with different morals and principles. Some are hardcore family men, while others are highly religious and devout people. However, there are a few men who believe in no morals or ethics but live by just one ground rule: *aurat aur daulat*—women and wealth.

Samad Khan, who was regarded as one of the most brutal operatives from the Pathan syndicate, changed the credo to a cruder form. He used to say, '*Yeh duniya mein sirf do cheezein hai dhanda aur danda* (This world has only two important things dhanda—business and danda—which usually means a rod but is also used as a euphemism for the phallus).' Khan was a sex maniac and was the most notorious womanizer in the underworld.

People who worked with him and knew him for a long time claim that Samad Khan could not survive without sex for more than three days. His addiction to sex was known to all his friends and fiends, his confidantes and combatants, his enemies and empathizers. Sex eventually became the cause of his downfall and destruction.

On that day, he craved sex. So much so that he could not concentrate on anything else. Impulsively, he made a call to Naseem, his new Kashmiri girlfriend, and fixed a meeting.

'Jaaneman, kaisi hai,' Samad asked Naseem. *'Mil mereko abhi* (Darling, how are you. Meet me now*)*,' he told her.

Naseem always met him in a hotel at Grant Road in the Sikka Nagar area of south Mumbai. As soon as Samad put the receiver down, Inspector Ishaq Bagwan, who had been intercepting the call, made his plan. Bagwan wanted to nab Samad as soon as possible and he thought this was the right opportunity. Bagwan immediately called his men and formulated a plan to take on Samad when he walked out of Naseem's house. He rushed to seek permission from his senior officer, who put a full stop to his plan.

The next day was Dassera, and Bagwan's seniors thought that the city needed a peaceful festival. Samad's arrest could lead to retaliation from other Pathan gangsters, and the police would have another headache to deal with.

Unaware of his enemies' machinations, Samad reached Sikka Nagar in a cab, which he stopped near a one-storey structure. As he took the steps to Naseem's room, his attention was diverted by five large baskets arranged prominently in a corner outside. The criminal that he was, Samad's observational powers were well tuned.

The incongruous presence of those big cane baskets at that spot made him pause, but not for long. The thought of undressing Naseem and plundering her cream-like curvaceous nude body disrupted his thought process. Samad only wanted sex at that moment. Nothing could stop him. He often joked that if someone set fire to his ass when he was in the middle of jackhammering strokes, he would not even feel the burning sensation until he ejaculated.

Samad rushed to Naseem's room like a hungry animal, almost tore off her clothes and made brutal and beastlike love. Naseem, he thought, was the most beautiful of all the women he had slept with. Her Kashmiri roots were evident in her fair skin which would turn a shade of pink. For him, Naseem was a beautiful distraction from the world of crime he lived in. Not for a second did he imagine that she might actually turn out to be an instrument of death.

Outside, the baskets started moving closer. At around six in the morning, as Samad was leaving, he noticed the baskets again. He saw that they had changed position. This time, since he had expended his sexual urge, he felt suspicious. He clutched his gun tighter, fearing that something was amiss. But before he could react, Dawood's hit squad, including Chhota Rajan, Babu Reshim, Sanjay Ruggad, Dilip Buva and Sunil Sawant, emerged from the baskets and fired a shower of bullets at him. The attackers were well aware that Samad was an early riser and had decided to target him when he was most likely to be caught off-guard. They kept firing at him till he had stopped moving.

Sawant, who was known as Sautya in the underworld, walked up to Samad's lifeless body, kicked him and fired another shot straight into his head. He then looked up at Naseem, who was patiently viewing the attack from her window, like a movie unfolding in front of her eyes. They smiled at each other in agreement. Naseem and the five attackers then disappeared from the area. The killers fled from the scene in three cars that were waiting for their return. While Samad's attackers went on to make their name in the underworld, no one ever heard of Naseem again.

Samad had only paid attention to two Ds—*dhanda* and *danda*. He should not have overlooked the third D—the most dangerous one: Dawood. Which eventually brought him to the fourth D—death.

Samad's death was as laden with bloodshed as his life was. According to the police, there were twenty bullets all over his body. His death came as a grisly climax to the mounting gang warfare between the Pathan group and the D-Company.

The Khans and the Kaskars

In those days, the Bombay underworld was divided in two groups: the Pathan gang, led by Amirzada and Alamzeb, and the D-Company. Both gangs had clearly demarcated their boundaries. The Pathan gang kept themselves busy by smuggling drugs along the Pakistan border, while Dawood's gang concentrated on smuggling through the Gujarat coastline. But despite the clear divide, there was bad blood between them. What started off with street fights later escalated into gangwars that painted the city red. Though Haji Mastan and Karim Lala, who were looked up to by the newbies, had managed to call a truce between the two warring gangs, the Pathans were said to have recanted on the agreement. Amirzada and Alamzeb used the opportunity to eliminate Dawood's brother Sabir.

On that fateful night in February 1981, Sabir was out to meet his girlfriend Chitra when he was caught unaware and attacked brutally in his car at a petrol station at Prabhadevi. Sabir was cornered by the Pathans and killed in gruesome manner. Dawood was shaken by his brother's murder, and when he saw Sabir's body, he swore to take revenge. From that day onwards, Dawood became the Pathans's nemesis; he wanted to annihilate the whole gang. In retaliation to Sabir's murder, Amirzada was shot dead in a crowded courtroom by Dawood's man David Pardesi in 1983.

Samad had not been part of Sabir's killing, and Dawood knew this. But he was a Pathan. And, more importantly, he was challenging Dawood's position in the underworld. Samad, along with his friends Shahenshah, Zia and Zuber, had dared to enter Dawood's stronghold in Pakmodia Street and unleash terror. The four had ridden their motorcycles through Pakmodia Street, firing bullets. Dawood's men did retaliate, but in the crossfire, Dawood's brother Iqbal Kaskar was injured. A bullet grazed his ear leaving him injured and bleeding profusely.

This did not go down well with the don. His ego was

hurt and his authority was challenged. Dawood was busy at his younger brother Anees' wedding ceremonies at the time, and was furious when he learnt about the daring attack in his area.

This was not the first time that Samad had directly crossed Dawood's path. Earlier, Samad had looted Dawood's consignment at the Mumbai docks. Dawood's smuggling activities were taken care of by his trusted aide Khalid Pehelwan. One day, when his consignment of gold and silver was about to land, Samad and his men entered the area and fired indiscriminately at the men waiting to receive the goods. Then they quickly loaded the crates and drove away.

Samad and Dawood's differences cropped up again over a plan to kill a hotelier. The hotelier was under Dawood's protection, and Samad—despite knowing this—accepted a supari to kill him. For Samad, his word was important. 'When a Pathan gives his *zabaan*, consider it done,' Samad would often boast. He finally honoured his word by killing the hotelier, thereby challenging Dawood and his supremacy yet again.

The final straw came when Samad assaulted on of Dawood's brothers, Noora, brutally beat him and inflicting major injuries that almost killed him

All these incidents enraged Dawood, but he knew that Samad was not just anyone who could be killed easily. Samad was merely twenty-eight-years-old when he earned the title of the most notorious criminal of Bombay. His Pathan connection, brazen attitude and fearless existence gave him an extra edge over the others.

After all, he came from the family of Karim Lala, the self-proclaimed don of the city. Samad was Karim Lala's nephew and he boasted of this relation anywhere and everywhere. Also, he himself was a fearless gunman and he also had a powerful team. His associates—Baba Khan, Mallad Khan, Jangrez, Karim and Sheru—were equally ferocious, and their ambition to take Dawood's position made them even stronger.

However, fortunately for Dawood, Karim Lala was not happy about the way his nephew used his name. Every time Samad committed a crime, Karim Lala was picked up by the police and held at the police station. It was quite humiliating for a man of his stature to get arrested for his nephew's crimes. A few months before Karim Lala severed his ties with Samad, he had a heated argument with his nephew, after which he publicly disowned him. The senior don put out an advertisement in a local daily announcing that he no longer had anything to do with his brother Rahim Lala's son Samad, and that his name was unnecessarily being dragged into controversies related to him. Karim Lala also announced that he would file a defamation suit against Samad if he continued with his behaviour.

Samad was heartbroken after he learnt about his uncle's decision. But he knew that he himself was to be blamed for this. Every time he became involved in a crime it was his uncle who would come on the police radar. Karim Lala was aging and was tired of being hauled to the police station, Crime Branch units and court rooms.

Karim Lala's announcement bolstered Dawood's

aspirations and provided the much-needed impetus to his plans. Karim Lala's protection had been an effective armour for Samad, and the reason behind his survival so far. Dawood addressed Karim Lala as chacha, meaning uncle, and his father Ibrahim Kaskar and Karim Lala were friends. Though Dawood wanted to kill Samad, he did not want to be directly blamed for the elimination. Initially, Dawood had even tried a counter-strategy: he had invited Samad to join his gang. But Samad was a staunch follower of the Pathan gang and the loyalist inside him would not budge. So Dawood had to come up with an alternative plan.

The Khatarnak Killer Khan

Samad was not just any other hit man. 'He was a ferocious monster who could take down twenty men alone. He was caught off-guard when he was killed or else he would have given a tough fight,' says Bagwan, now retired from the police service. Samad's price was reportedly between one-and-a-half and two lakh rupees for one supari—quite a high price for the early '80s. Perhaps the most expensive hitman of his time. But he was considered too volatile, too trigger-happy and often too indiscreet for his own good.

Police records reveal that he was connected with twenty killings, the last being when he fired two rounds from a moving car at a man named Iqbal who was sitting on the bonnet of another car.

A month earlier, he had shot a passport agent at Santa

Cruz. Later, he was arrested for the brutal murder of Texmaco senior executive S. K. Jain at Sea Rock Hotel. Samad had been given a contract to eliminate a Birla executive with the last name of Jain. Through his trusted informers, he found out that Jain was residing in Sea Rock and was supposed to check out soon.

He decided to kill Jain in his hotel room. As he walked into the hotel's reception, he felt out of place at first. Samad was better off in the dingy lanes of south Mumbai rather than this posh hotel. He asked the receptionist for the room number in which Jain was lodged. The receptionist told him that it was against the rules of the hotel to divulge any information about a guest. Samad took out his revolver and placed it on the table and then looked at the receptionist again. She hurriedly scanned the register and told him it was 1921. Samad picked up his revolver and left the hotel. He waited for night to fall so that it would be easy for him to do his job without attracting attention.

Around midnight, Samad, accompanied by two others, marched into the hotel lobby and took the elevator to the nineteenth floor. When he knocked on the door, it was opened by a middle-aged man who looked at Samad in surprise. '*Kya re, Jain. Bahut neend ho gayi. Chal time pass karte hai,*' said Samad and pushed him inside. Jain tried to protest but he could do little. Samad sat on the sofa and asked his men to continue. Both his men started bashing up Jain. They pinned him to the ground and went on hitting him for some time till Samad asked them to stop. He then asked the man to strip in front of them. As Jain got up he saw that Samad was pointing his revolver at him and thus had no choice but to oblige. After stripping he was asked to dance to Bollywood songs. This torture continued till morning, and when it was dawn, Samad got up, removed his belt and strangulated the man. All three then left the hotel room.

The next day, Samad saw in the newspapers that the Jain he had killed was a Texmaco executive, and his full name was S. K. Jain, not Ranveer Jain, who he had been assigned to kill.

Samad was filled with rage as he had a reputation to live up to. He was known to get his target in a single attempt. As a result, he then went to Sea Rock again the next day and this time killed Ranveer Jain, accomplishing his mission in style.

In 1981, he was accused of killing a man while trying to get him to sign the sale deed for a flat. In 1983, in the month of August, Samad staged a daring escape from his police escort in the compound of the city civil court. The shooter had hatched a plan with his then girlfriend Shilpa Zaveri. She was a very good driver and no one could catch up with her if she was behind the wheel. That morning, when Samad was brought to the sessions court, Shilpa was waiting in her car at the corner of the road. While Samad was being released on bail in one case, another police team was waiting across the road to re-arrest him in another case. As soon as Shilpa saw the cops escorting him out of the court, she pressed on the accelerator and drove at a top speed towards the police party. When they saw the car rushing towards them they jumped aside for fear of being hit. Only Samad continued to stand where he was. Just as the car was about to hit Samad, it came to a screeching halt. Samad immediately jumped into the front seat and Shilpa sped away. This time she took a U-turn and came back where the other police party was waiting. They waved good-bye to the cops and fled away.

Shilpa had pulled off the stunt so well that the police had very little time to respond. The police tried to pursue them but could not match Shilpa's speed and ability to manoeuvre the vehicle. Samad was so impressed with Shilpa that he soon married her and began living with her. However, his desire for other women led to cracks in the relationship and it is suspected that it was also Shilpa who tipped off Dawood about Samad's location when he was killed at Sikka Nagar.

Samad's most outrageous act was when he was lodged in the central jail in Bombay during 1983–84. Samad knew that most of the men in the jail were Dawood's men and he had to be very careful. But even that did not stop him from calling the shots. He controlled the prison as if he owned it. Even the jail authorities danced to his tune. He was given all the facilities, like a television set, hot water to bathe with and his favourite chicken biryani whenever he demanded. He carried out his extortion business from within the jail. Samad's freedom depended on two witnesses, and if they turned hostile, there would be no case against him. Samad got his men to bring the two witnesses to meet him in the jail. Once there, Samad handed over a razor to each of them and asked them to shave their head, moustache and eyebrows. When they refused, he summoned the jail barber to get the job done. This, Samad told the two men, was simply a warning. 'If you speak one word against me in court, you will suffer worse,' he warned them. 'Next time, the razor will be at your necks.'

As he wanted, the two witnesses turned hostile and charges against Samad were dropped. This was not the first time that Samad had walked free from the clutches of the law. Despite the police making a strong case against him, he always managed to stay out of jail. Samad was twice detained under the stringent National Security Act (NSA), but managed to be freed by the advisory board. He also managed to obtain bail in half-a-dozen murder cases for which he was arrested.

Rama aur Rum

In 1972, a wealthy Bombay resident opened the first dance bar in the city, named Sonia Mahal. The bar was in the Nariman Point area and it was where one could find all the attractions—women, alcohol and music. Top businessman, diamond merchants and criminals—Sonia Mahal became a hangout for all. The concept was simple: cleavage-showing women would take centrestage and move their bodies to Bollywood songs; the restaurant area would have a seating space from where men could enjoy their drinks and enjoy the alluring sight of the women. Bollywood-watchers say that Feroz Khan's idea of a bar dancer in his hit movie *Qurbani* was inspired by Sonia Mahal. In fact, Zeenat Aman's character in the movie was named after the most attractive girl in the joint.

The city buzzed with this popular line, 'Rama aur Rum', meaning that dance bars offered women as well as alcohol. In the shady corners of the dance bar, deals would be signed or broken. Gradually, the rowdy elements increased and Sonia Mahal and other dance bars that came up one after another would be frequented only by them. It was in Sonia Mahal that the first fight between Dawood's brother Sabir and Pathan gangsters took place. The police found it tough to maintain law and order here but then it was also a 'source of income' for them.

On most days, one could find two heavyweights of the crime world enjoying their drinks in the bar, Samad Khan and his ally Anjum Pehelwan. Often completely inebriated but still drooling over the girls, Samad would beckon them to his table. As the girl walked towards him he would try to catch hold of their hands and pull them towards him. *'Kya bhaav khaati hai. Chal na,'* he would say. The women in the dance bar knew how to deal with these clients. They would resist at first, extract enough money and then give in. Samad would often bet with Anjum on a particular girl that he wanted to take to bed that day.

There was one girl Samad had already tried to take to bed. He had showered her with a lot of cash but she refused to oblige. She was the daughter of a railway employee and had joined the dance bar to earn more money. Samad had been watching her for a few days, but the girl continued to ignore him. One day Samad and Anjum pounced on the girl, lifted her in the middle of her performance and took her out of the bar. No one dared to stop them.

Samad took the girl to the flat of his mistress in Versova and raped her repeatedly. Anjum stood guard outside the room, drinking. Later, Samad stepped out and went away with Anjum. Meanwhile, the girl's father, who had already found out about her kidnapping, approached the Colaba police station. Inspector Ishaq Bagwan and his colleagues were on night duty at that time. As soon as they heard Samad's name they jumped from the seat and proceeded to Versova. Bagwan knew exactly where to find the duo. When they entered the flat they saw the girl weeping in the room. They sent her away for medical examination and went to the spot where Samad and Anjum were sitting and enjoying their drinks. Both were arrested and put behind bars. Samad did not resist the arrest as he knew that the cops could do little to keep him in jail for long.

And, as expected, he walked free in a few days as the girl refused to give a statement or file a police complaint against the gangster. No law could keep Karim Lala's nephew behind bars.

The Most Dangerous D

Dawood was a master planner and he knew his enemies' weaknesses. Dawood knew Samad would stoop to any level to get a woman to sleep with him. And that, Dawood believed, would bring about his end. There were other options to target Samad. For example, Dawood could simply tip-off the police and Samad could be killed in an encounter. But then that would not make any statement for the D-Company. Hence, Dawood thought of a bait. A bait that Samad could not resist.

Dawood meticulously planned Samad's death. He did not want to be predictable by using a bar girl to lure Samad as there was also a chance that Samad's loyalists would tip him off. So he called for a new girl from Delhi. Dawood's orders were simple: find a good-looking girl in need of money. One of his men found Naseem, who readily agreed to work for him. Naseem was then given a job in a dance bar where Samad was a regular. The instructions to Naseem were that she should only lure Samad and no one else. Soon, Samad fell for this beauty and he could not think beyond her. At times he would wonder how this beautiful woman liked an unkempt man like him. But then he would tell himself that he was a Pathan, and any woman would fall for him.

Naseem knew that if Samad got even a hint of her intentions, he would kill her. But Dawood had promised to protect her. After the attack, she was to be sent off to a safe location and would never again be contacted by Dawood or his men, the don had promised her. And, she would be given enough money to last her lifetime.

Soon the courtship began. Samad would meet his new 'item' at different locations. He would make love to her and send her off. Naseem waited patiently for Samad to get used to her and trust her. Eventually, Samad fixed a location where they could meet every time.

On the eve of Dassera, Naseem decided to tip off Dawood. She knew Samad would not suspect anything.

Mumbai underworld's smartest killer was silenced because of his craze for women. On 4 October 1984, Samad was killed in more or less the same manner as Sabir Kaskar. Helpless, cornered by an entire gang and riddled with bullets till the last breath.

Samad's killing concluded a particularly gruesome chapter in Mumbai mafia history. Karim Lala was distraught and his anger against his nephew did not hold him back from attending Samad's funeral along with over two thousand others, including personalities like Muslim League MP G. M. Banatwala, and filmstar Dilip Kumar's brother Ahsan Khan.

All fingers were pointed towards Dawood and the don finally decided to escape from Mumbai and shift his headquarters to Dubai. Over the next decade, between 1984 to 1994, no one could challenge Dawood's numero uno position in the underworld. It was only much later that Chhota Rajan threw the gauntlet down, but according to cops who knew Samad, it was undoubtedly this Pathan who had the ability to become the unmatched king of the mafia world. With his death, Dawood safeguarded his position and remained invincible till the emergence of the Rajan–Arun Gawli alliance.

EPILOGUE

Gunmen's Gaffes

In my thirty years of covering the crime beat in Mumbai, there have been a lot of takeaways. Like the realization that courage has its own definition, as elastic and nebulous as its own garb. Some policemen get puffed up in uniform but others don't need khaki to show their nerve. Ditto the criminal. The guts and glory comes from the little metallic contraption hidden in their pockets for most, others could command a legion of supporters across the board by exuding charm.

Anything contradictory to this, that is, pure black and white terms, works only in the realm of celluloid as depicted in Bollywood where there are no grey shades, no in-betweens, where the definition of courage means a conscientious younger brother in uniform in a witch hunt for his older brother who is on the other side of the legal fence.

In the real world, not all the gunmen are sharpshooters. In fact, some of them could not even shoot straight. Both Husain and I, in our combined journalistic careers, have not come across anyone who was gifted with guns. They could only shoot at pointblank range. The weapon made them feel invincible, as well as access to the big don; at other times, they were aided by external forces. Like the time when Amirzada got bumped off in a Mumbai sessions court by David Pardesi.

When Dawood wanted to avenge the killing of his brother Sabir, he was on the lookout for an assassin who had the mindset of a suicide bomber. Somebody who knew at the outset that the mission could fail and he could lose his life. Amirzada had killed Sabir at a petrol pump in Prabhadevi. Dawood wanted the Pathan dead, not out in the open or behind the still darkness of the night. But in broad daylight in a court room, while the trial procedure was in progress! The assignment was well nigh impossible.

Nobody was ready to take on the assignment despite the promise of a mouthwatering compensation. Finally, Dawood found a man who was willing to take on the job. His name was David Pardesi. He was lazy, unambitious, a loafer from the Chembur area in north-eastern Mumbai. His days passed without any aspiration to do anything at all. So Pardesi thought the best way to tackle his ennui was to accept Dawood's challenge.

Dawood gave Pardesi guns to practise at a shooting range at Ulwe near Uran. He offered him fifty thousand rupees for killing Amirzada in the court premises. It was the highest payment ever made for a supari in those times. You could buy four huge flats for that amount. And yes, Pardesi managed to shoot Amirzada dead but with a little help. The twist in the tale. He got a little push from a man in uniform who cannot be named. Dawood trusted Pardesi to do his job but knew that, in a courtroom, he would need help.

Over the years, I have seen some of the men in khaki do unspeakable things, things that might make the mafia's shenanigans look sissy. But then they were shielded by their uniforms. While it gave them immunity, it shed their moral fibre.

The mafia, on the other hand, were sometimes a befuddled lot. There is an interesting tale of a fellow called Umar Asif Shaikh from the Abu Salem gang. Back in the late '90s, Umar earned the reputation of being one of the daftest in his tribe.

Umar was assigned the task to extort money from a jeweller in Pydhonie area in south Mumbai. For Umar, it was a promotion. From being a weapon-delivery man, he was being pitched into *hafta wasuli* or extortion. Enthusiastically, he landed up at the jeweller's shop without doing the mandatory recce. Umar entered the shop after the customers and staff had left and confronted the jeweller with his gun. 'Give me all your money or I will shoot you dead,' Umar threatened the jeweller. The jeweller was used to mafia threats but this one seemed not to follow the line. 'I don't have any money to give. Shoot me if you wish. As it is my business is in doldrums, it is better to die than to live like this,' the jeweller burst out in defiance but with a tinge of depression in his voice.

Since the threat to kill was already made, Umar felt that not shooting the man in his first assignment itself would make him a laughing stock. The gun was already pointed, so Umar held the gun closer to his victim's head and aimed to shoot.

The jeweller closed his eyes and thought of God, waiting for the flying bullet to blow his brains. Umar summoned all his anger and pulled the trigger.

Seconds ticked away. Nothing happened. Then an ugly sound of '*khat*' echoed in the shop.

The jeweller opened his eyes, realized he was still alive and saw a look of bewilderment on the shooter's face.

Suddenly the jeweller surmised that his maker wanted him to live. He looked around and saw a small rod lying near his feet. With lightning agility, he picked up the rod and struck at Umar's head. The youth plummeted to the ground. The cops were summoned and Umar was arrested and thrown behind bars.

Encounter specialist Pradeep Sharma, who killed 111 gangsters in the twenty-five years of his police service, explained the fiasco in layman's terms. Often shooters fail to check if the gun is in a working condition. Either the bullets don't fire as they are spoilt over a period of time. Or the firing pin is bad and the hammer will not strike. In this case, it was simply that there were no bullets: the shooter had picked up the pistol in a hurry, and had not checked if the magazine was loaded or not. An experienced gunman would have felt the difference in weight.

So when Umar pulled the trigger, the empty chamber made a sound indicating that it had a void and could not fire.

Umar spent several months in jail smarting from the

embarrassment. The utter failure in his maiden assignment had made him the biggest joke in the underworld. So he spent every waking hour in jail devising ways to kill the jeweller whom he held responsible for his fiasco. After his release, he would complete his unfinished business and salvage his tattered reputation.

After spending over six months in the slammer, Umar was released. Within a couple of days of his release, Umar decided to take revenge. This time he decided to be thorough. Umar procured the gun, ensured that the magazine was full, and did some dry runs. When he was confident, Umar landed up at the shop again.

The shopkeeper was initially nervous to see the man but immediately regained his composure. Umar, on the other hand, was visibly tense and on tenterhooks. The jeweller decided to placate him and negotiate with him. '*Achcha beta,* I will give you *dus thaan* (ten thousand rupees) today and next month I will give you another installment.' Thaan means thousand in mafia slang.

Umar was angry. A silent fury was raging in his frail frame. Months had passed but he had not gotten over his humiliation. He wanted blood as a recompense for his insult.

'*Aaj mujhe tere thaan nahin teri jaan chahiyye,*' growled Umar and whipped out his pistol.

The jeweller seemed resigned but decided not to cower. He would take his chances. '*Theek hai beta, maar de mujh ko chala goli,*' he said with a tone of resignation in his voice.

Umar trained the gun and pulled the trigger. And

again nothing happened. In desperation, Umar began to pull the trigger repeatedly, hoping for the gun to sputter to life.

Before Umar could act, the jeweller picked up his metallic cash box and threw it at the bumbling gunman and raised an alarm. The neighbours heard the call for help, gathered there and bashed up Umar and handed him over to the police. This time around, he spent a considerable time at the J J Hospital nursing his wounds before being packed off to the jail again.

Sharma explained that every Chinese-made semi-automatic star pistol of .30 bore has to be cocked, the barrel needs to be slid backward for the bullet to be primed and ready to fire. Perhaps Umar forgot to cock the gun or he simply did not realize that the lock was still in place. 'One should always cock and unlock before you shoot,' Sharma said.

A famous underworld adage is, *Ghoda ghode se nahin goli se marta hai.* You can't kill a horse by merely pointing a gun at it, the trigger should be the bullet that will kill the horse. 'Ghoda' is gun in underworld slang.

In his late twenties, Umar Asif was known to be a romantic man and carried his heart on his sleeve. He often masqueraded as a poet and tried to impress girls with his poetry. To this end, he had an agnomen added to his name. He called himself Umar Dhadkan (the heartthrob).

His tryst with the jeweller of Pydhonie who lived twice to tell the tale, got him a new title. Umar was nicknamed as Umar Dhakkan (the doofus). The nickname was a metaphor for his stupidity, which he brought forth in his laughable encounters with the jeweller.

This incident seemed to me to indicate how mafia hitmen have become vestiges of a bygone era, of a time when guns were glory for the underworld. With most of the lethal and dangerous hitmen dead, or languishing behind bars, they are now a vanishing tribe, thankfully.